WHEN THE
SPIRIT
COMES WITH
POWER

Signs & Wonders among God's People

JOHN WHITE

INTERVARSITY PRESS
DOWNERS GROVE, ILLINOIS 60515

InterVarsity Press is the book-publishing division of InterVarsity Christian Fellowship, a student movement active on campus at hundreds of universities, colleges and schools of nursing. For information about local and regional activities, write Public Relations Dept., InterVarsity Christian Fellowship, 6400 Schroeder Rd., P.O. Box 7895, Madison, WI 53707-7895.

Distributed in Canada through InterVarsity Press, 860 Denison St., Unit 3, Markham, Ontario L3R 4H1, Canada.

All Scripture quotations, unless otherwise indicated, are from the Holy Bible, New International Version. Copyright © 1973, 1978, International Bible Society. Used by permission of Zondervan Bible Publishers.

Cover illustration: Michael Goss

ISBN 0-8308-1222-9

Printed in the United States of America

Library of Congress Cataloging in Publication Data

White, John, 1924 Mar. 5-
   When the spirit comes with power.

   Bibliography: p.
   Includes index.
   1. Revivals.   2. Experience (Religion)   3. Holy
Spirit.   I. Title.
BV3790.W472   1988   248.2'9   88-6841
ISBN 0-8308-1222-9

17	16	15	14	13	12	11	10	9	8	7	6	5	4	3	2	1
99	98	97	96	95	94	93	92	91	90	89	88					

To Lisa my daughter-in-law and Susan my grandchild

Acknowledgments

I am grateful to many people whose kindness has made this book possible. I cannot name all who allowed me to interview them. They were most patient, tolerating my prodding, my needling, my repeated requests for clarification. Those whose stories appear in part two were especially patient.

John Wimber made it clear to me that I had free reign in conducting inquiries among the members and staff of the Vineyard Christian Fellowship in Anaheim, and encouraged me to monitor the conferences he conducted. He and his wife Carol, along with Sam and Gloria Thompson and other members of the pastoral staff at the Vineyard Christian Fellowship in Anaheim, gave me every assistance in finding out whatever I wanted, supplying me with address lists, telephone numbers and suggestions about whom to approach.

In Argentina Carlos Annacondia and Rev. Omar Cabrera graciously allowed me to spend time with them, answering all my questions and welcoming my observations. Dr. Philemon Choi put me in touch with the Chinese Church Research Centre in Kowloon Tong, Hong Kong. Mike Pinkston in Dallas did some excellent research for me. And many other friends, knowing of my interest, made helpful suggestions. To all these brothers and sisters I owe many thanks.

My daughter Liana went over some of the manuscripts, meticulously sorting out typos, while Lorrie my wife was as patient as she always is when I lock myself up to quarrel with my computer for hours on end. However, I cannot and shall not blame any of them (even my temperamental computer) for defects in the final product. As authors sometimes put it, I, and I alone, am responsible for any goofs.

Part I
The Spirit's Power in Revival

1
What in the World Is God Doing?

THESE EFFECTS ON THE BODY WERE NOT *owing to the influence of example, but began . . . when there was no such enthusiastical season as many account this, but it was a very dead time through the land."* JONATHAN EDWARDS

"We must be very careful in these matters. What do we know of the realm of the Spirit? What do we know of the Spirit falling on people? What do we know about these great manifestations of the Holy Spirit? We need to be very careful 'lest we be found fighting against God,' lest we be guilty of 'quenching the Spirit of God.' " D. MARTYN LLOYD-JONES

John, a British preacher, spoke at a meeting in a Baptist church in Penang, Malaysia. Afterward several Chinese Christians asked him to pray for them. He did so, first inquiring of each one in turn what his or her need was.

The first man said, "I tremble a lot, especially when I'm scared. I'm scared of the boss at work. When he yells at me I tremble. I was trembling while you spoke."

John thought he had been gentle in his address but, determined to help the man, he asked that God would by his Spirit enable the man to overcome his fears. As he prayed the man began to tremble. When John saw what was happening, he prayed more earnestly, whereupon the intensity of the trembling increased. The man was shaking rather than trembling.

"Is this the trembling you are talking about?" the preacher asked.

"Yes."

"And you tremble when you are afraid?"

"Yes."

"Are you afraid now?"

"Oh, no. This is wonderful. I feel a great peace."

"You mean this is different from what happens to you at work."

"Oh, yes!"

The second man did not tremble. He jerked his limbs this way and that as the preacher prayed.

"Why are you jerking your legs and arms?"

"I don't know. I just am."

"Has this ever happened to you before?"

"No, never."

The third was a woman in her twenties. She requested prayer because though she had daily devotions for many years, God always seemed remote and distant from her, and she was discouraged. This time John prayed sitting beside the woman, and as he prayed she began gradually to slide off the seat.

"What is happening to you?" he asked.

"I'm sliding off the seat," the woman replied.

John's wife held her to keep her from collapsing onto the floor as her body continued to slump.

"Thank you so much," the woman said. "The Lord is so close. I've never realized his presence like this before."

As John reflected on the meeting and what happened afterward, it occurred to him that it was all the more unusual because the people at the meeting were controlled, disciplined Christians to whom such behavior was unknown.

Steven stood staring at the man in the foyer. "Who is he?" he thought to himself. "I know him from somewhere. I just can't place him." Suddenly, with a stunning realization, he recognized him. He was a friend Steven had known years ago, a friend who was disfigured and crippled by a badly distorted spine. But the man Steven stared at was well and could walk without a limp. As Steven spoke to him, his old friend told him he had been made well at the conference they were both attending.

That was the beginning of a new era in Steven's life. During the worship time at that same conference Steven would regularly find himself weeping. People would tell him that "the Holy Spirit was all over him," but Steven had no such impression. However, at a later conference in Ohio, as he was leaving the pastors' meeting one lunch time, he "heard the Lord tell him to stop and to stare at a certain man." He continued to do so for several minutes, to the evident consternation of the man concerned. No reason was ever given for this mysterious instruction, if such it was. However as he stared, the Holy Spirit's power descended on Steven. He was uncertain what was happening, since his legs became unmovable while his body began to feel heavy, as though he were drugged. He closed his eyes. Bewildered, he found himself swaying, felt he was going to fall and thought he heard the Lord tell him not to worry, that he would not do so.

By this time he was not sure whether he was asleep or awake, but sensed people gathering round him and praying. Then as he began to fall backward he was laid on a row of seats by the people around him. He felt ashamed, feeling he ought to get up since there were "so many things he ought to be doing for the Lord." Into his heart came the words, "No, this is your time. Open your heart."

He experienced a sensation as if he were melting into the chairs. He had no clear sense of time but was told he lay there for about forty-five minutes. During that time Steven saw in his mind the Lord reach down to where he was lying and pluck his heart from his body, saying, "That's no good. You'll never do anything with that." Then the Lord plucked his own heart from his chest and put it inside Steven's body, saying, "There! You can do something with that!"

Steven wept brokenly, his body shaking violently, and he cried, "Lord, I love you so much—and I can't believe you love people as much as that!" To which the Lord replied, "Now get up—and eat!" (He had not eaten for three days.)

He got up from the chair, still feeling the weight of the Lord's presence. When he began to move, "it was like slow-motion football." Feeling sure that the Lord's presence was "on him" for some purpose, he walked across to a hospital close by, and after eating lunch there, visited a couple of the patients, who were both healed as he laid his hands on them and prayed for them.

The following day all sensation of "heaviness" had left him, so that he was uncertain whether the "magic" of the previous day would still "work." However, since that time, though his own expectation of anything happening is small, he has continued to lay hands on people in need, often with powerful and surprising results.

Steven's experiences and visions had a profound impact on his life. Lack of parental affection while growing up and the scars of a divorce had left him full of despair and self-loathing. But these had given way to joy and to a renewed desire to minister to others and to bring them to Christ.

Carlos Annacondia is a pentecostal evangelist in Argentina who is known for conducting his many citywide *conquistas* (conquests)—what we would usually call crusades. These are character-ized by the use of open fields accessible to public highways, excel-lent lighting and amplification systems, large tents for inquirers. He attracts huge crowds, especially on weekends. He is also known for his cooperation with whatever churches in an area invite him to work with them. He does not restrict himself to pentecostals. Often he is opposed by a number of groups—by Macumba priests (a powerful Brazilian cult representing a mixture of African magic with some Roman Catholic practices), by witches, by followers of the Jehovah Negro (another Brazilian cult) and even by groups of *curanderos* (who treat the sick with herbs and spells). Through a variety of disruptive techniques, they have tried to break up his meetings. Independent witnesses confirm the presence of occult practitioners in the meetings.

Attempts have even been made on Annacondia's life by such people. In San Martin on May 5, 1985, one man on the outskirts of the crowd fired five times at Annacondia, using a high-powered rifle with telescopic sights. The same night, complete with rifle, the man was drawn into the body of the meeting and fell to the ground under the power of the Holy Spirit, confessing that he had been "sent by the Black Jehovah to murder" the preacher. A member of the local police prayed with him but did not arrest him. The would-be assassin appeared to be converted, but was never seen again.

Asia. North America. South America. These are three stories that I know about personally. I could also recount episodes from Africa and Europe. And there appear to be hundreds, if not thou-sands, of similar occurrences around the globe. What does it all mean? What are these reports of extreme emotional reactions and unusual behavior currently observed around the world among Christians of various theological persuasions—reports of great weeping or laughter, shaking, extreme terror, visions, falling (or what is sometimes called "being slain in the Spirit"), being "drunk with the Spirit" and other revival experiences? Something is certainly going on, and that something seems potent. Is it revival? Is it from God?

We must be cautious in evaluating new religious movements. Many new movements are mediocre and a few, extremely dangerous. False fire burns fiercely, an angel of light still spreads his wings, and the elect continue to be deceived.

Too often, however, we rely on rumor to determine what is going on. Sometimes our fear causes us to condemn too quickly, especially concerning something new and spectacular. But is there a baby in the bath water? God himself has been known to act spectacularly so that there is always a danger of missing him in our skepticism. He is still at work in the world.

We would be wise to adopt a more open skepticism and to be willing to go to the trouble of investigating some movements firsthand. But if we do, by what criteria shall we evaluate?

Since I had the opportunity to investigate current events for myself, I felt a responsibility to do so, knowing full well that I see only dimly. During recent travels in Asia, Latin America, England and North America, I gleaned all the information I could about revival movements there, discussing cases with the leaders I met.

I also accepted an invitation from John Wimber to spend a year in California, observing the nature of the Vineyard movement, meeting with the leaders, observing the life of the Anaheim Vineyard and interviewing at great length many people who had experienced the kind of manifestations described by Edwards, Whitefield, Wesley and some of the nineteenth-century evangelists in camp meetings in the United States.

I suppose that as a psychiatrist I have brought the weaknesses as well as the observations and skills of my profession to this task. And certainly I have brought the curiosity of a psychiatrist about unusual behavior. But my aim has not been to write an encyclopedia of bizarre behavior. Rather it is to widen the perception and encourage the discernment of my fellow believers, pointing out what I hope is the right direction.

In doing all this, I have had to grapple with people's experiences, past and present. In this book I have given a great deal of space to accounts of those experiences. Some readers may feel I spend too much time on experience and not enough time expounding Scripture. Nevertheless I make no apology for devoting so much space to descriptions, and have a purpose in so doing.

It would be different if my only aim were to prove something. In that case the criticism would be valid. But as a trained psychiatrist I value data on human reactions. Part of my purpose is to present data. This can be quite helpful, for example, to pastors who may be called on to evaluate the experiences of some members of their congregations. This is not always an easy task.

Thinking a problem through to some extent before one encounters it in the flesh can be valuable. Though I have traveled widely and made observations for a number of years, I have limited the descriptions in this book largely to the English-speaking world, and to events of the last three or four years. Even so there is too much material to discuss in detail.

Further, I have limited my discussion to unusual emotion and behavior. While I believe that divine healing is part of the ministry of the church, I shall not discuss it in detail. The reason? I want to make sense of the behaviors that have been a feature of revivals past and present. And healing has not always been associated with all revivals. Therefore, while some accounts I give will include references to healings, glossolalia and other "charismatic" manifestations, my object is not to express an opinion about these or to convince anyone of their genuineness. Like any manifestation of spiritual power, in themselves they prove nothing. I include them only where they are integral to an understanding of a particular manifestation and where the account of it would otherwise be incomplete or misleading.

We can, however, be unnecessarily fearful, particularly of things like supernatural healing, and we should heed the words of Puritans of the past. Richard Baxter, for instance, once wrote: "I know men's atheism and infidelity will never lack somewhat to say against the most eminent providences, though they were miracles . . . but when mercies [i.e. of healing] are granted in the very time of prayer, and when, to reason, there is no hope, and without the use or help of any other means . . . is not this as plain as if God from Heaven should say to us: I am fulfilling to thee the true word of my promise in Christ my Sonne? How many times have I known the prayer of faith to save the sick when all physicians have given them up as dead!"[1]

My book has three sections. Part one focuses primarily on strange behavioral manifestations themselves and their relationship to revival. Chapter two examines Scripture and history to see what they can teach us about these issues. The next two chapters consider the negative reactions revival has usually received in history. Chapters five and six ask whether the revival experiences are merely psychological, or even demonic, or else of God. Chapter seven describes the commonest of the many forms of manifestation, and the following chapter tries to make sense of the differences among them, inquiring why (if they are genuine) one person might fall on the ground, another tremble and a third cry out. The last two chapters of this section look more carefully at the dangers associated with focusing on these experiences excessively, and in particular at the question of Satanic power.

The chapters in the second section are devoted to detailed case histories of people who have experienced manifestations of one form or another, and the effects their experiences had on their lives. The last section discusses the relevance of all this to our lives here and now.

I do not present any final answers. My psychiatric experience is helpless before some of the phenomena I encountered. Jonathan Edwards's words express what many of us feel, whether one is an examiner of such phenomena or is the subject of them: "And it has been very observable, that persons of the greatest understanding, and who had studied most about things of this nature, have been more confounded than others. Some such persons declare, that all their former wisdom is brought to nought, and that they appear to have been babes, who knew nothing."[2]

So this is a book about the reality of revival and about the particular significance of certain manifestations in revivals. In the past these were deplored by believers and unduly emphasized by others. I do not want to pull back from anything God might be doing. And I fear that some of us, not understanding what is happening, may miss the joy of seeing God work in power and of being with him in what he is doing. Others, on the other hand, seem so enamored of anything spectacular that they neglect standard means of grace, such as the study of Scripture and intercessory prayer.

So, both as a psychiatrist and as a Christian, I have examined what is taking place and want to share my findings and tentative conclusions with my fellow Christians. There is much at stake. We are here only once. Earth affords opportunities that eternity cannot. I want to help fellow Christians not to miss collaborating with God in revival through fear and undue fascination or misunderstanding.

2
Has It Ever Happened Before?

WHEN CHRISTIANS ENCOUNTER A question they don't know how to answer, one of the first things they should do is ask another question—namely, What does the Bible have to say about this? And that is an excellent question to ask about special experiences of God and the unusual behaviors that are sometimes exhibited at various Christian gatherings around the world.

When Heaven Comes Down
The answer is that the Bible has a great deal to say about such issues. We might divide the material into several categories. The first consists of encounters with the divine that produce mental and

physical changes, usually temporary, but sometimes permanent.

God is, of course, present everywhere. But there seem to be times when he is, as it were, more present—or shall we say more intensely present. He seems to draw aside one or two layers of a curtain that protects us from him, exposing our fragility to the awesome energies of his being. Even the presence of an angel can cause bodily failure.

Daniel collapsed in terror when Gabriel appeared to him. A trancelike sleep overwhelmed him. As Gabriel approached him he was conscious, yet powerless to move. "And I heard a man's voice from the Ulai calling, 'Gabriel, tell this man the meaning of the vision.' As he came near the place where I was standing, I was terrified and fell prostrate. . . . While he was speaking to me, I was in a deep sleep, with my face to the ground. Then he touched me and raised me to my feet" (Dan 8:16-18).

The physical effects of this encounter, even with supernatural enabling to stand, were extreme. Our minds and bodies can stand only so much. "I, Daniel, was exhausted and lay ill for several days. . . . I was appalled by the vision; it was beyond understanding" (Dan 8:27).

On another occasion, several hundred years later, the disciples heard the voice of God on the Mount of Transfiguration. "They fell facedown to the ground, terrified. But Jesus came and touched them" (Mt 17:6-7). Luke also tells us (9:32) that they had been drowsy just previous to this. Why were they drowsy? Were they bored because Christ had been praying for a while? That was what happened later in the Garden of Gethsemane.

But think about it. There came a point when they saw his face change (and at least one of them must have observed it happen to record it) and his clothing become "as bright as a flash of lightning." What would that do to their drowsiness? No. The drowsiness must have an unusual explanation. Later I shall discuss the heaviness that comes over some people when the Holy Spirit's power rests on them—a drugged, almost drunken stupor.

John describes his vision on Patmos in similar terms to Daniel's. "When I saw him, I fell at his feet as though dead. Then he placed his right hand on me . . ." (Rev 1:17).

On the three occasions when the Lord has appeared to me personally I experienced some of these overwhelming effects. What happened was something I have never sought and did not expect but can never forget. On the first two occasions I was somehow able to remain kneeling, in spite of appalling weakness and trembling. I mumbled adoration and confessions incoherently between my sobs. On the third occasion I lay on my face, a quivering mass of adoring jelly. I, therefore, am unable lightly to dismiss what I see of certain phenomena in the present, or what I read about in the past.

The Shaming of King Saul

We would be mistaken, however, if we were to suppose that extraordinary experiences mark God's favorites or that they are a sign of superior spirituality. Two contrasting passages in 1 Samuel describe what happened to Saul. On both occasions the Holy Spirit caused him to prophesy for an extended period of time. On the first occasion he was blessed, but on the second he was humiliated and left hardened in sin.

The first passage shows us Saul in his youth. He is returning home after his first encounter with Samuel. Samuel has anointed him as the future king and has predicted his future. Among other things Samuel tells him, "The Spirit of the LORD will come upon you in power, and you will prophesy with them; and you will be changed into a different person" (1 Sam 10:6).

As he continues his journey he is met, as Samuel predicted (10:5), by a company of prophets following a group of musicians, and prophesying (in chorus?) as they walk. As soon as they meet, Saul is overwhelmed by a powerful anointing of the Holy Spirit, (". . . the Spirit of God came upon him in power . . .") and he begins to prophesy in the same manner as the prophets (10:10).

The passage seems to focus on the awesome power of the Spirit which causes Saul to do something he has never done before, and that probably astonishes Saul as much as people who observed him. His acquaintances are watching and their surprise is clearly caused as much by what they saw (10:11) as by what they heard.

It seems likely that the Spirit's power produced discernible (possibly ecstatic) changes in the prophets, changes the people observing Saul were familiar with. The effects of the Spirit's power evidently lasted for some time (10:13).

Something is happening to Saul that strikes the onlookers as the genuine article—as the same thing that occurs to the prophets when they are under the Spirit's power. So they ask the question, "Is Saul also among the prophets?" Was his father a prophet? (The prophetic tradition was frequently passed from father to son—Amos 7:14.)

As for Saul, he has been anointed with oil and by the Spirit and has been prepared for his future kingly role. But there is another lesson we must learn. The Holy Spirit's anointing is no guarantee of superior spiritual performance. Tragically, Saul's personal ambitions lead to the removal of God's anointing, and the preparation does him no good.

Years later Saul has a second and less felicitous encounter with the Holy Spirit's power (1 Sam 19:15-24). David has escaped Saul's murderous designs and is in Naioth at Ramah with Samuel and a group of the prophets. Saul sends men to capture him, and when they arrive they also encounter the prophets in full voice under the power of the Holy Spirit.

In what might be called a power encounter, God strips every vestige of power from Saul's followers. Divine power overcomes them and all they can do is join in the chorus of prophecy (19:20). Clothed with the power, the soldiers are paradoxically thereby rendered powerless—stripped, as it were, of the king's power by a greater power.

On learning what has happened, Saul sends two more delegations who encounter the same fate. Finally he proceeds to Naioth himself. On his way there the Spirit of God comes on him, and like a puppet on a string he prophesies until he arrives. And just as his men have been stripped of power, so the king is stripped of his robes and lies naked on the ground before Samuel, prophesying all that day and on through the night (19:23-24).

The Spirit of the Lord does not honor Saul. It humiliates him, shaming and rendering him impotent, totally unable to exert his will in the presence of his foes. His stubborn heart rejected God's mercy.

Therefore when the power took effect it mocked his pride and kingly power. Manifestations of the Spirit's power do not ever reflect credit to the person in whom they are manifest. They reflect only the power, the glory and the mercy of God, whether the manifestation results in the subject's blessing or the subject's humiliation. They can never be a ground for boasting.

They are never a sign of God's favoritism or of superior spiritual attainment.

Revivals in the Bible?

A second category of experiences can be labeled revivals. Did revivals occur in Scripture? And if they did, were behavioral manifestations (what Wesley called "signs and wonders") a part of them?

Revivals were not called by that name in Scripture, but they are described. For instance, in Nehemiah 8 we find the people of Jerusalem spontaneously pour into the Water Gate square requesting Ezra to give them a reading of Scripture (8:1).[1]

They do not gather in response to organized publicity. The narrative gives no explanation for their request. We may assume the Holy Spirit is behind it and that prayer has played some part. But usually the Holy Spirit uses people to affect his work. Was it perhaps the examples of Ezra and Nehemiah that had awakened such an outpouring of yearning for God's law to be read?

We are told twice in the next few verses that the crowd was made up of people who were able to understand (8:2-3). In the culture of the day that meant adults of both sexes and males of twelve years or more. However, the main point is the exercise was intended not to arouse passions but understanding. Levites were stationed some distance from each other and from Ezra, repeating and interpreting what was read for the benefit of those who could not hear. The arrangements, strange as they may seem to us, were designed to be educational, not to get people worked up. They were designed "so that the people could understand what was being read" (8:8).

Yet in spite of the purely didactic aim, there was a dramatic emotional reaction. Spontaneously the crowd broke into lamentation and weeping (8:7-9). It could not have been due to psychological manipulation by Ezra and Nehemiah for two reasons. First, the reading arrangement was so clumsy. Second, Ezra and Nehemiah were themselves distressed by the weeping. In alarm they and the Levites tried to calm the people, telling them that rejoicing is more appropriate (8:10).

Even so, it was no mere flash of emotionalism. The genuineness of the revival is evidenced in its lasting results. First, the people insisted on reviving the Feast of Booths (8:13-17), a harvest festival that made them aware not only of God but of their history of being guided by God into the Promised Land. Second, during the Feast, Ezra continued to read from the scroll and the people fasted and gave themselves to public prayer (9:1-3). In the end the whole nation made a solemn and binding agreement. Common people, priests and leaders all commited themselves, under a curse, to keep the law of Moses (10:1-29) and to rectify failures immediately (10:30-39).

The Spirit of God had intervened. He has brought about renewal and a profound change of heart and vision among the Jews. They are now set on the true course of national destiny.

The events described in the earlier chapters of the Acts also parallel events that we now refer to as revivals or awakenings. For one thing, the apostles themselves were behaving in a remarkable way—preaching the gospel fluently in a variety of languages that had not been previously stored in their brains. They were accused of drunkenness, but the accusation surely did not arise from their speaking strange languages. If you come across a man speaking fluently in a foreign language, even if it is not your own language, you don't suspect he's been drinking too much. No, the appearance of drunkenness which evidently affected some of them was a phenomenon we shall look at later.

Then again there are the changes in the listeners. Luke says they were "cut to the heart" (Acts 2:37) after they heard Peter's sermon on the morning of Pentecost. It seems that the whole multitude of three thousand people were affected, evidently displaying agitation and clamoring round the apostles in their distress to demand a solution.

I am reminded of a passage from Jonathan Parsons during the Great Awakening: "Under this sermon many had their Countenances changed: their tho'ts seemed to trouble them, so that . . . their knees smote one against another. Great numbers cried out aloud in the anguish of their Souls."[2]

And as was the case in the days of Nehemiah, the revival was more than a temporary emotional outburst. Rather, the changes God worked took hold as the church flourished throughout the known world.

Modern Parallels

Throughout history, too, men have described sensations similar to those found in Scripture. Blaise Pascal, the seventeenth-century philosopher and mathematician, made the following notation in his journal about his experience from about half past ten in the evening until half past midnight on Monday, November 23, 1654: "Fire. 'God of Abraham, God of Isaac, God of Jacob,' not of philosophers and scholars. God of Jesus Christ. God of Jesus Christ. My God and your God."[3] There follows an incredible outpouring of words in Pascal's vain attempt to describe the indescribable.

Charles Finney, the great nineteenth-century American evangelist, described an overwhelming experience of God as "waves of liquid love." Later in the century, another evangelist, Dwight L. Moody, also struggled to put his encounter with God into words. One problem is that many people to whom such things occur are reluctant to talk about them because of the sacredness and intimacy of the occasions. Descriptions are frequent, but the language restrained. In Moody's case it was

. . . one day, in the city of New York—oh, what a day!—I cannot describe it, I seldom refer to it; it is almost too sacred an experience to name. . . . I can only say that God revealed himself to me, and I had such an experience of his love that I had to ask him to stay his hand. I went to preaching again. The sermons were not different; I did not present any new truths, and yet hundreds were converted. I would not now be placed back where I was before that blessed experience if you should give me all the world—it would be small dust in the balance.[4]

Early in this century, Evan Roberts, the leader of the Welsh revival, received many visions and vivid experiences of the divine presence. In 1904 he underwent a profound anointing of the Holy Spirit in Blaenannerch. He went back to his home in Loughor and began to hold prayer meetings which in a matter of days drew larger and larger crowds as revival swept the whole region. After one such meeting, Roberts wrote, "After many had prayed, I felt some living energy or force entering my bosom, restraining my breath, my legs trembling terribly; this living energy increased and increased as one after another prayed. Feeling strongly and deeply warmed, I burst forth in prayer."[5] (Some Christians claim that Roberts subsequent interactions with Jesse Penn-Lewis convinced him of the diabolical nature of his experiences, but their arguments are not very convincing, and I know of no documentation supporting their view.)

Such experiences as these is what Martyn Lloyd-Jones called the baptism of the Spirit. In a series of sermons now published under the title *Joy Unspeakable*, Lloyd-Jones used the term not in a modern sense, but in a sense steeped in the biblical understanding of the English Puritans. To him it meant an anointing or enduing with power, sometimes, but not usually coinciding with conversion, often repeatable, intended for all the church, dramatic, experimental, observable and connected only indirectly with sanctification.

Revivals in History

We have found so far that history provides many examples of Christians who had many intense experiences of the divine similar to those found in Scripture. What can we say about revivals in church history as compared to those in Scripture? Let's take a closer look.

Even as a child my imagination was gripped by accounts of revival. I did not understand all I read, but I knew I had found my heart's true home. I treasured my big, battered copy of John Wesley's journal. My pulse would also quicken over stories of the Welsh and the early Korean revivals.

Later, while I was on leave from the navy during World War 2 and touring the Scottish highlands with a Christian friend, I met two Hebridean Islanders. Their glowing faces and anointed lives told their story more clearly than their musical but broken English. It was a story of singular beauty, holiness and power, the story of what was then occurring in the Hebrides.

Much later an address by Duncan Campbell confirmed their story of fishermen who as their boat passed the island were constrained to pull into harbor. Knowing nothing of the revival, the men had been so overwhelmed by a spontaneous conviction of sin that they could proceed no further. At least so the story went. Later reports suggested that that particular account was part of a growing Hebrides mythology.

What is more certain is that miners would drop their tools and fall to the ground in anguish over their sins. From such stories it seemed that the Holy Spirit had enveloped the island in an invisible cloud that changed human thought and behavior radically.

It reminded me of the time when Jonathan Edwards, the eighteenth-century pastor, preached his sermon, "Sinners in the Hands of an Angry God." I can see him in my mind's eye in his pulpit, reading his sermon shortsightedly as he peered at the manuscript by candlelight. He must have been charged with passion. But his reedy, high-pitched voice would hardly qualify him as a dynamic preacher. It was the power of God, not erudition or eloquence, that gripped church members that night. The building rang with echoing cries of terrified listeners, men and women clutching the pillars of the building with all their strength, terrified that the floor would split, and their feet go slipping and sliding into hell.

Edwards was just one of many preachers who contributed to the Great Awakening in the American colonies in the mid-1700s. George Whitefield, the English evangelist, probably had more to do with the wide spreading of evangelical faith and repentance in Christ than any other single person. But the Great Awakening was more than a one-person campaign. It affected dozens of cities and hundreds of congregations.

Sydney Ahlstrom says of the Great Awakening in New England: Flamboyant and highly emotional preaching made its first widespread appearance in the Puritan churches (though by no means in all), and under its impact there was a great increase in the number and intensity of bodily effects of conversion—fainting, weeping, shrieking, etc. But we capture the meaning of the revival only if we remember that many congregations in New England were stirred from a staid and routine formalism in which experimental faith had been a reality to only a scattered few. . . . Preaching, praying, devotional reading, and individual "exhorting" took on new life. In spite of far more demanding requirements, the increase in church membership is estimated variously between twenty and fifty thousand. . . . Equally certain is the fact that the Awakening had many far-reaching, even permanent, results . . . [in] the social and political legacy of the revivals.[6]

One major difference between the Great Awakening of the eighteenth century and the current awakening concerns the attitude to miracles and so-called charismatic (or "sign") gifts. Edwards accepted manifestations but was cautious about visions and rejected healing miracles. He felt strongly that emotional impressions must be distinguished from prophetic revelation. Whitefield recognized the validity of initial manifestations but opposed any encouragement of them. In his earlier years he was prone to attach significance to "impressions" he received from God. Edwards and Whitefield even talked about the issue of "impressions" on one occasion, Edwards urging Whitefield to abandon them.

As we move ahead in our look at revival, let me try to pull together in a preliminary way some general conclusions. First, regarding terminology, *revival* and *awakening* are sometimes distinguished, the one referring to what happens among Christians and the other to what happens among the unconverted. I shall use the term *revival* to cover both. What we have called revival during the last three hundred years represents an unusual work of the Holy Spirit with the following characteristics—

1. Converted and unconverted men, women and children, stunned by a vision both of God's holiness and his mercy, are awakened in large numbers to repentance, faith and worship.

2. God's power is manifest in human lives in ways no psychological or sociological laws can explain adequately.

3. The community as a whole becomes aware of what is happening, many perceiving the movement as a threat to existing institutions.

4. Some men and women exhibit unusual physical and emotional behaviors. These create controversy. They can be an offense to opponents of the revival and a snare to its supporters.

5. Some revived Christians behave in an immature and impulsive way, while others fall into sin. In this way the revival appears to be a strange blend of godly and ungodly influences, of displays of divine power and of human weakness.

6. Wherever the revival is extensive enough to have national impact, sociopolitical reform follows over the succeeding century.

In this way Christ's kingdom begins to be exercised over the evils of oppression and injustice.

Revivals are like forest fires, varying in their extent and influence. They seem to begin in several places at the same time. Here in Canada we sometimes hear the radio or TV reporting a serious situation where a hundred or more forest fires rage at the same time. The nightmare in the firefighters' minds is that these fires will coalesce. Each of the smaller fires is itself a picture of a small revival. But there are some revivals that resemble a coalescing of many fires. (One of these, the Great Awakening of the eighteenth century, I see as central in formulating a definition.)

Why do many people who pray earnestly for a visitation from God reject what he sends because they find it offensive? What can we say about the bizarre behavior that occurs, the unwise words and actions of its prominent leaders, the bitter quarrels that arise? How shall we avoid the tragedy of missing it when God sends it? These are the questions we will begin to answer in the next chapter.

3
Revival Rejected

T HEY HAVE GREATLY ERRED IN THE WAY
in which they have gone about to try this work, whether it be a work of
the Spirit of God or no . . ." JONATHAN EDWARDS
"This is no age to advocate restraint; the church today does not need
to be restrained, but to be aroused, to be awakened, to be filled with a
spirit of glory, for she is failing in the modern world." D. MARTYN
LLOYD-JONES

From a safe distance of several hundred years or several thousand miles, revival clearly looks invigorating. What could be more glorious than a mighty work of God in our midst, renewing thousands and converting tens of thousands.

But when we actually look at a revival (either through close historical study or firsthand investigation) we find something not nearly so clear as we imagined. There is sin and infighting and doctrinal error. And if we find ourselves in the midst of revival, rather than being invigorated, we may be filled with skepticism, disgust, anger or even fear. Why does our expectation not match the reality? Why is revival sometimes so messy?

The Ebb and Flow of Battle

One reason is that revival is war, and war is never tidy. It is an intensifying of the age-old conflict between Christ and the powers of darkness. When we read the Old Testament we occasionally become aware that there are visible and invisible events in Bible history. The conflict between Israel and heathen nations surrounding them represents the visible end of a wider spectrum, the invisible end of the battle having greater significance than the visible. This becomes clear when the invisible soldiers and their captains cross the line, briefly crashing the sight barrier, so to speak.

One day Joshua is startled by a confrontation with the "commander of the LORD's army" (who may well be the preincarnate Son). God speaks through him giving Joshua precise battle plans for Jericho (Josh 5:15—6:5).

In 2 Kings 6 we find that two armies, one visible and the other invisible, surround the city of Dothan and the person of Elisha. Only as the eyes of Elisha's servant are opened can he see "horses and chariots of fire." The intense reality of the invisible war, and likewise the significance of prayer, become clearer yet in the vision Daniel receives of the heavenly warfare that is about to take place (Dan 10:1—11:1).

But we may ask: Didn't Christ already win the victory? Can war in the spiritual realm have any meaning now that Christ has forever defeated the powers of darkness? Isn't the war over? And isn't the victory won primarily in the sphere of the lives of Christian believers?

Let me begin with the last question first. In what sphere does Christ's victory operate: only in the life of believers and by extension in the church? Or do his claims to rule extend over the whole earth? Here there can be only one answer. Throughout the Old Testament, Yahweh makes it clear that he is the God of all nations, the Creator of the earth and all creatures in it.

Even at the Fall, God never abdicated that claim, which is repeatedly emphasized by the prophets. Psalm 2, seen as referring to Jesus by the writer to the Hebrews (Heb 1:5), asserts that God's anointed one will rule the earth with an iron scepter (Ps 2:7-12). And John the apostle quotes from the same psalm, asserting that the enthroned Jesus would rule all nations with an iron rod (Rev 12:5).

Satan anticipates this rule of Christ when he offers him "the kingdoms of the world and their splendor" (Mt 4:8-9). The Satanic rule began at the Fall when man invited it by sinning and when the divine curse instituted it. But Satan's rule is more analogous to a usurper's rule. Christ's kingdom *(basileia)* means his rule, the effective nature and sphere of his authority. He comes to reestablish it—and that by conquest.

But was that conquest not complete at Calvary? How shall I express it? Let me put it this way: *The war was won, but the fighting goes on.* Christ is already the victor. He wears a victor's crown on his head. By his incarnation, death and resurrection he has struck the final blow against the powers of hell. He has disarmed them and publicly humiliated them (Col 2:15). At the shout of his triumph the temple curtain was ripped apart, the earth shook, rocks split and the dead burst out of their tombs (Mt 27:50-53). That is why the gates of hell cannot and will not prevail against his church. But the end is not yet.

Oscar Cullman tries to explain the paradox in terms of the Second World War. He sees the Normandy landings as a sort of equivalent to Calvary, in the sense that the world knew that when the Allies had landed successfully in Normandy, that the war was at an end—finished. The Allies had won. But the German High

Command refused to accept reality and in their psychotic denial, fought on. Indeed the bloodiest fighting of the war followed.[1]

Hell's powers are equally insane. Doomed and hopeless, they fight on in spite of Calvary. Our own battle against them is real. We do not beat the air. We wrestle against principalities and powers (Eph 6) while angelic hosts fight alongside us. From time to time cosmic mopping-up operations achieve other breakthroughs, what we call revival occurs and the invisible side of the picture seems for a time to become more apparent.

Knowing that revival is like war and like a forest fire (which we mentioned in the last chapter), doesn't necessarily make revival easier to understand. Even the godliest person who in an unguarded moment puts on spectacles of envy and pride, will see only human error and confusion.

To recognize a divine visitation we must view it through twin lenses of discernment and humility. It is easy to recognize it in books or in retrospect since we are usually accepting the view of the writer of a particular history. To recognize it when it occurs is more difficult. During the revivals of the past three hundred years, many Christians were too confused by their wrong expectations to perceive what God was doing. And so firm were some in their rejections that I suspect they would not have believed even had the dead returned to convince them.

Revivals can also be compared to new movements in society like a reform movement or a revolution. Such movements commonly arise when they embody an emphasis or an idea whose "time has come." The movement's emphasis corresponds to a felt need, a sort of thirst for what the movement offers. Into an ideological and emotional vacuum a revolution is birthed, and the greater the vacuum, the more significant the revolution. Pushed too far, a new spiritual emphasis becomes heresy. But if the Holy Spirit continues to refine the doctrines, a great movement of God emerges, a movement that has wide-ranging effects on society as a whole as well as on individuals in it.

The Seamy Side of Revival

That was the case with the nation of Israel in Nehemiah 8—10. The whole fabric of society changed as God began to exercise rule over the evils of oppression and injustice. The same was true as a result of the Great Awakening. Nonetheless, not all evils were corrected nor, as Jonathan Edwards saw, were all sinners made sinless.

Critics seized on inconsistencies, but Edwards's dictum was: "A work of God without stumbling blocks is never to be expected."[2] In fact he said: "It is no sign that a work is not from the Spirit of God, that many, who seem to be subjects of it, are guilty of great imprudencies and irregularities in their conduct. We are to consider that the end for which God pours out his Spirit, is to make men holy, and not to make them politicians. It is no wonder that, in a mixed multitude of all sorts—wise and unwise, young and old, of weak and strong natural abilities, under strong impressions of mind—there are many who will behave themselves imprudently."[3] He also wrote: "Instances of this nature in the apostles' days are innumerable . . . gross heresies . . . vile practices. . . ." [4]

He was right. We do not dismiss Paul's ministry in Corinth because the Spirit's movement there was subsequently associated with gross sexual indecency and with affronts to the body of Christ at the Lord's table. Nor do we deny the divine inspiration of Peter's epistles because of his compromises with the Judaizing party. (Did any of his contemporaries ask, "How can you take the guy's preaching seriously after the way he behaved in Antioch?") We must be cautious about dismissing a movement if its leaders make mistakes or its followers fall into sin and error.

George Whitefield, the real leader of the Great Awakening, lived to regret and publicly berate himself for his intemperate assaults on the churches of his day: "Alas! alas! in how many things I have judged and acted wrong. . . . I have been too bitter in my zeal. Wild-fire has been mixed with it, and I find that I frequently wrote and spoke in my own spirit, when I thought I was writing and speaking by the Spirit of God."[5]

Modern leaders have been molded from the same clay and are subject to the same temptations as were Whitefield and Peter. If we fail to look beyond their failings we may not spot what is happening round them. In our preoccupation with human weakness we may fail to see what God is doing.

Scorching Words

The irony of revivals is that while they are so longed for in times of barrenness, they are commonly opposed and feared when they arrive. Revivals represent the normal activity of the Holy Spirit with increased magnitude. "I would define a revival," writes Martyn Lloyd-Jones, "as a large number . . . being baptized by the Holy Spirit at the same time; or the Holy Spirit falling upon, coming upon a number of people assembled together. It can happen in a chapel, in a church, it can happen in a district, it can happen in a country."[6]

This increase in the Spirit's activity provides other reasons for our often less than enthusiastic endorsement of revival—it disturbs the community. Church dignitaries are particularly offended by two things. They deplore "hysterical behavior" in religious meetings. They also resent new leadership. Since revival is often characterized by both, vested interests within the church react with fear and hostility.

Opposition to revival comes not just from sinners but from Christian leaders, some of them godly and respected leaders. And in this sense, revival causes division. The hostility is never to the idea of revival, which is ardently prayed for, but to God's answer to our prayers and the unexpected form it may take.

The more articulate the leaders were, the more colorful their language became. Some leaders changed their views in time, for time makes issues clearer. But during the battle, the dust obscured the view and the noise drowned out the sound of the trumpet. Unfortunately, colorful expressions survive.

Ralph Erskine was a godly and astute thinker, greatly used by

God in a revival in Scotland (which included many unusual manifestations) in the early eighteenth century. However, when Whitefield visited Scotland, even though a warm friendship by mail had developed between himself and the Erskine brothers, the Erskines urged him to join the Associate Presbytery, desiring to set him straight "about the matter of church government," including the errors of the Church of England.

Because Whitefield could not agree to do as they wished, the friendship ended. The Associate Presbytery vilified him in 1742 in a pamphlet entitled *The Declarations, Protestation, and Testimony of the Suffering Remnant of the Anti-Popish, Anti-Lutheran, Anti-Prelatic, Anti-Whitefieldian, Anti-Erastian, Anti-Sectarian, True Presbyterian Church of Christ in Scotland.* In it they charged that "Whitefield's foul prelatic, sectarian hands" had administered the sacraments to Presbyterians and stated that Whitefield "is not of a blameless conversation. . . . but is a scandalous idolater. . . . a limb of antiChrist; a boar, and a wild beast. . . ."[7] The love and warmth was gone. Spring had turned into the scorching heat that eventually brings drought and death.

Let us beware of condemning the Erskines. They were outstandingly godly men. Not only does the intemperate tone of their pamphlet reflect historical circumstances and usages, but also the wounds inflicted by terrible persecutions of their Covenanter forefathers. Who of us knows our heart's dark depths? And when our bitterness is expressed in words, the words can go on doing their damage for generations. Many examples of the same intemperate language, only slightly more moderate in tone, continue to this day.

Earlier in the twentieth century, the fear of pentecostalism gave rise to verbal firecrackers. One leader called pentecostals the "rulers of spiritual Sodom," their tongues "this Satanic gibberish" and their services "the climax of demon worship."[8] The phrases suggest carnal anger more than godly fear. While glossolalia may indeed be inspired by demons as well as by the Holy Spirit, it can be harmful to write books with such titles as *Demons and Tongues*—a 1936 diatribe against the early pentecostals.[9]

G. Campbell Morgan referred to pentecostals as "the last vomit of Satan," while R. A. Torrey accused them of being "founded by a sodomite."[10] When we are excited and afraid, none of us is immune from intemperate outbursts.

J. B. Simpson was more gracious, adopting for the Christian and Missionary Alliance a "seek not—forbid not" policy, eventually known as the "Alliance position."[11] Torrey and Campbell Morgan never lived to see the subsequent development of the pentecostal movement, or their words might have been more charitable.

Vitriolic expressions have also erupted periodically through the lips of holiness and pentecostal leaders. Each side has the tendency to limit the word *revival* to examples of it which satisfy a particular theology or ecclesiology, ignoring or even explaining away what God does in another camp. Pentecostals tell stories of Wesley and glory in Azusa Street. Calvinists quote Jonathan Edwards and remember Whitefield and Spurgeon. Godly leaders in both camps are human beings, sometimes (like all of us) unaware of the true reasons for their personal windows on history and of the sources of their prejudices.

We grow angry when we are scared. We fear what we cannot understand. True revival has commonly been opposed because it came dressed outlandishly, a wild and uncouth invader. Each revival had its own style, its own novelty.

Field preaching, for example, was unheard of in Britain before the Wesleyan revival. Churches and chapels were scandalized initially. Press articles describing it scorched the paper they were printed on. When George Whitefield first introduced him to it, even John Wesley found field preaching hard to accept. His journal entry for March 29, 1739, reads: "In the evening I reached Bristol, and met Mr. Whitefield there. I could scarce reconcile myself at first to this strange way of preaching in the fields, of which he set me an example on Sunday; having been all my life . . . so tenacious of every point relating to decency and order, that I should have thought the saving of souls almost a sin, if it had not been done in a church."[12]

Such fears plague us all. Novelty throws us and troubles our consciences. Fortunately for England, Wesley's temperamental rigidity and punctiliousness were exceeded by his longings to advance with God. He refused to be blinded or bound by tradition. He displayed daring and humility, boldly following the trail Whitefield had blazed through unsafe territory along unconventional paths, rather than clinging to safety, to familiar sounds, phrases, routines.

Older people find change particularly difficult. Edwards, noting how older people react in revival, warns those of us whose arteries are hardening (a category that includes many senior Christian leaders): "There is a great aptness in persons to doubt of things that are strange; especially elderly persons."[13]

But if revival comes with eruptions of burning hostility, it also brings with it a new openness of heart among members of the family of God. Friend George, a Quaker, told George Whitefield in 1741, "I am as thou art; I am for bringing all to the life and power of the everliving God: and therefore if thou wilt not quarrel with me about my hat, I will not quarrel with thee about thy gown."[14]

Whitefield shared the same spirit. In preaching the gospel he was not ashamed of being contaminated by others. The threat of "guilt by association" never daunted him. Faced with bitter criticisms such as that of Ralph Erskine he writes, "I was more and more determined to go out into the highways and hedges; and that if the pope himself would lend me his pulpit, I would gladly proclaim the righteousness of Christ therein."[15]

With Decency and Order?

Some fear is good. Wild things may be perfectly safe, but wildness is a criterion neither of safety nor of godliness. The bizarre can be dangerously evil. And in the twentieth century we have been warned by the tragic examples of Jim Jones, David Berg and Sun Myung Moon. Destructive cults exist.

But fear can make us paranoid. It can paralyze us, turning us into toothless armchair critics instead of soldiers. We become like the servant who so feared his Lord that he hid his talent in the ground so his business venture would not wind up in catastrophe and his lord be enraged. When we are afraid we should examine what is happening for ourselves, carefully and at first hand. Are we scared of noise? of disturbances in meetings? of excess? George Whitefield once wrote of his participation in the famous revival in Cambuslang (1742):

Such a commotion surely was never heard of, especially at eleven at night. It far outdid all that I ever saw in America. For about an hour and a half there was such weeping, so many falling into deep distress, and expressing it in various ways . . . their cries and agonies were exceedingly affecting.

Mr. McCullough preached after I had ended, till past one in the morning, and then could scarce persuade them to depart. All night in the fields might be heard the voice of prayer and praise. Some young ladies were found by a gentlewoman praising God at break of day. She went and joined with them."[16]

Excessive religious emotion can be worrying. Tongue in cheek, Lloyd-Jones once cried, "Fancy upsetting the clock-like, mechanical perfection of a great service with an outpouring of the Spirit! The thing is unthinkable!"[17]

In days gone by we used to talk about religious mania. As a psychiatrist I have seen many psychotic states which take a religious form. Edwards (who referred to emotions as "affections") pointed out that: "Though there are false affections in religion, and in some respects raised high: yet undoubtedly there are also true, holy, and solid affections; and the higher these are raised, the better. And when they are raised to an extremely great height, they are not to be suspected merely because of their degree, but on the contrary to be esteemed."[18]

What is it that scares us? Fear of error? Or of not being in control? In the Chronicles of Narnia, C. S. Lewis tells us, "Aslan is not a tame lion." By that he seemed to mean that God is neither predictable nor controllable. True, he is a God of order, a God whose almighty word made chaos and darkness take their flight, but bringing in order is sometimes a disorderly process. It is neither tempest-free nor routine. Chaos and darkness flee, but they create a ruckus as they leave.

Understandably we prefer peace. And for us peace has to do with structure and tranquility. Both are good, but our desire for them has led us to confuse order with quietness and predictable schedules, and to believe we have the former when we have achieved the latter. Commenting on the New England revival in the early eighteenth century Edwards wrote: "Some object against it as great confusion, . . . and say, God cannot be the author of it; because he is the God of order, not of confusion."[19]

For Edwards, order could be accompanied by the turbulence and noise of men and women crying out for pardon, or falling on the ground and shaking, or even of "the devil crying out with a loud voice." He considered it no more confusion than "if a company should meet in the field to pray for rain, and should be broken off from their exercises by a plentiful shower."[20]

So convinced was he of our folly in deploring "confusion" when the Holy Spirit is at work that he cried: "Would to God that all the public assemblies in the land were broken off from their public exercises with such confusion as this the next sabbath day! We need not be sorry for breaking the order of means, by obtaining the end to which that order is directed. He who is going to fetch a treasure, need not be sorry that he is stopped, by meeting the treasure in the midst of his journey."[21]

The criticisms of the early methodists, of Whitefield and of many past revival movements have sometimes been based on a wrong notion of order. The accounts of them abound with descriptions of people weeping, shaking violently, crying out, losing consciousness, falling down and sometimes becoming uncontrollably agitated. It is a mistake to encourage such behavior. One reason is that encouragement inspires insecure people to imitate it. But the behavior can occur spontaneously, and regularly. All calm goes out of the window with the first scream. And with the first scream we question not only the propriety of the disturbance, but its source.

John Wimber writes: "When warm and cold fronts collide, violence ensues: thunder and lightening, rain or snow—even tornadoes or hurricanes. There is conflict, and a resulting release of power. It is disorderly, messy—difficult to control."[22]

He further says: "Power encounters are difficult to control. This is a hard word for many Western Christians to accept, because phenomena that do not fit rational thought are uncomfortable: they plunge us into the murky world of the transrational in which we lose control of the situation. Events that do not fit our normal categories of thinking are threatening for us, causing fear, because they are unfamiliar—especially where spiritual power is involved."[23]

Russell Spittler points out in an unpublished paper that in the early periods of revival in North America since the mid-eighteenth century only one, the Moody-Sankey period, lacks unusual behavioral manifestations. (Though Synan points out that speaking in tongues did accompany Moody's preaching on occasion.)[24] A similar assertion can be made of revivals in Britain.

If we insist that revival must be "decent and orderly" (as we define those terms) we automatically blind ourselves to most revivals. Like the dwarfs in C. S. Lewis's children's story *The Last Battle*, we may spit out heavenly food, for to us it looks like, smells like, tastes like dung and straw. Revival stirs our hearts when we read about it. But would we perceive it as of God if it broke out noisily in one of our own services or meetings?

Fear of the New Breed
Revival brings other offenses. Revivals spawn their own leaders.

Then comes a general bristling of whiskers among the old guard and its supporters. There are two sources of discontent. First, the clergy-laity distinction becomes blurred, threatening clerical institutions. Second, emerging leaders may lack formal training and social polish.

Yet has God ever limited himself to highly educated people? He raised up judges to deliver Israel, one or two of whom were distinctly offbeat. The prophets included an assortment of poets, scholars and unlettered men. Jesus, himself a carpenter, chose what some people would regard as a motley and lightweight bunch to found the church with. Paul noted that he and his followers were perceived as "the scum of the earth, the refuse of the world" (1 Cor 4:13).

Years ago Martyn Lloyd-Jones, lamenting the spiritual condition of his native Wales, gave a lecture deploring the modern tendency to value a person's words by the number of degrees he or she possessed. "What degrees," he asked, "had Daniel Rowland, Howell Harris, William Williams, John Elias?"[25]—all evangelists who had profoundly shaped the national character of Wales.

Whenever the kingdom advances, the front line is perceived as scum. There is a sociological as well as a spiritual explanation of this. Christian movements have proved to be powerful in the degree that they have captured the hearts of the poor—for God goes for the rabble. Thus the new breed of Christians generally includes a disproportionate number of people seen as the social inferiors of the religious establishment. There are exceptions to the rule, but in general Anglicans and Presbyterians regarded early methodists as Johnny-come-latelies. North American Methodists in turn could look down on pentecostals, not only for their doctrine and practice, but for the social origins of their members, drawn as they often were from the lowest ranks of society. The gospel had been preached to the poor.

Many kinds of fears cause people to turn their backs on revival. We have looked at several in this chapter. But one more fear remains. It is a fear so widespread among Christians, especially Western Christians, that it deserves a chapter on its own. And that is the fear of emotions.

4
Should We Fear Emotions?

WHEN WE READ THE HISTORY OF RE-
vivals conscientiously, we read about some pretty unusual behavior in revival meetings. Of these the easiest to understand are expressions of emotion. Yet even manifestations of emotion present
us with problems. Christianity concerns faith. It is faith that saves
us. So where do emotions come in?

The Story of Faith, Feelings and Facts
In my youth as a Christian I was greatly helped by the story about
Faith, Feelings and Facts, companions together along a tricky path-
way. The first two followed Facts who was in the lead. The story
taught me that objective truth (Facts) was what mattered, and that

my eyes of faith should be pinned on the facts, rather than on my emotions. Mr. Faith, you may remember, was often bothered when Mr. Feelings got into difficulties. However, when he took his eyes off Facts and turned to help Mr. Feelings, he himself invariably got into difficulties until he remembered that his job was to follow Facts, not to worry about Feelings. And according to the story, sooner or later Feelings would catch up.

The story teaches both a truth and a lie. The truth is that our faith is based on facts, not on feelings. The lie was that feelings always caught up.

I learned about the lie from a neighbor. I counseled Maggie to keep on following the truth about her salvation. But her feelings never caught up with her faith even after years of heeding my oft-repeated story. Eventually she committed suicide in despair. It was only then that I began to reflect more carefully on the somewhat simplistic story.

For one thing, it is possible to be mistaken about the facts since Mr. Facts really represents one's own limited understanding of Scripture. It is always possible for our own grasp of facts to lead us astray, unless we are open to revise or refine it from time to time. And again, feelings are complex. Faith is only one of many factors influencing them. After all, if something so ordinary as a missed night's sleep or a bout of indigestion can affect them, what else might?

As I grew up, there was an unspoken rule in my home that we were not to express strong emotion. We loved one another dearly, but we tended not to kiss or hug one another. Self-control extended to all excessive expressions of warmth. Quietness and order also characterized the gatherings in our Plymouth Brethren assembly. Classical hymns were sung in a restrained manner at the "morning meeting" and gospel hymns (a little mournfully) at the gospel meeting on Sunday evening. Prayers were earnest but no one either became enthusiastic or broke down and wept in prayer. If any misguided visitor shouted, "Hallelujah!" children turned round to stare while their seniors pretended not to have noticed.

Yet in such a setting I learned to respect and to love Scripture. I also learned in the depth of my spirit (even though worship involves the villain of felt emotion) what true worship was about. Yet to this day, psychologically sophisticated as I may be, I feel uncomfortable with people who emote too much around me. I am trained, to be sure, to react with appropriate warmth to whomever emotes. But some of my discomfort remains. It is cultural and not spiritual discomfort. It was a product of the fears and behaviors of my environment.

I was warned against Holy Rollers and Quakers. I suppose the warnings had their origins both in a concern for false emotion (in which religion has always abounded) and concern for doctrinal error. Both concerns are important. Nevertheless I am stuck—and perhaps will remain so to the end of my days, with an unhealthy degree of discomfort in the presence of strong emotion. And I suspect I am far from a solitary case.

Years of careful research into our emotions has made it clear that while careless giving way to emotional impulses can be harmful and destructive, many of us are sick, and some of us ultimately die because of repressed and overcontrolled emotions. They inflict horrendous damage on our cardiovascular and gastrointestinal symptoms. High blood pressure and ulcers of various kinds are closely linked with emotion. It is likely that there is not a bodily ailment which is not connected in some way with our hidden fears, our unexpressed griefs and our inability to rejoice without restraint.

And what better place could there be for the release of our pent-up emotions than before the throne of grace? Why can some Christian leaders scream with delight or howl with rage at football games but never think of shouting "unto God with the voice of triumph"? Our Christian culture has too often made it difficult for us to "shout for joy and be glad" even when it would be appropriate to do so. In fact I ask myself: Are most conservative Christians scared of emotion? If so, why? We should be scared of emotionalism, the artificial manipulation of emotion. But emotion itself? Let me lay down the basic principle.

Emotion comes from seeing, from understanding. I experience fear when I realize I might die during the operation the surgeon has suggested to me. The depth of my fear measures the clarity with which I see. My fears will be healthy if what I "see" truly corresponds with reality, for emotion is a test of my grasp of reality. Emotions do not save me—except in the sense that they may startle and shake me into acting in the light of truth.

When the Holy Spirit awakens people, he seems to cause them to perceive truth more vividly. Satan's deceptive mists are driven away. People see their sin as terrifying rocks threatening to sink them or as a foul, stinking cancer that will kill them. They see the mercy of the Savior with the eyes of those who have been snatched from a horrible death. Their trembling, weeping and shouts of joy reflect the clarity of their vision.

Keenly aware of this, Dallimore states that the emotional manifestations we are talking about took place in people who were "solemnly conscious of the presence of God . . . and bitterly aware of their own helplessness."[1]

The Parallel Tracks of Will and Emotion
Perhaps no one has written more wisely about emotions than Jonathan Edwards. Between 1740 and 1745 Edwards grappled with all that was happening in the revival in New England, seeking to integrate it with what he understood of Scripture.

Edwards believes teachers are in great error if they "are for discarding all religious affections, as having nothing solid or substantial in them."[2] Well aware that heat and light must go together, he urged that we need more than mere knowledge. We also need "holy affections," by which he means emotions within God's will. "The Holy Scriptures everywhere place religion very much in the affections; such as fear, hope, love, hatred, desire, joy, sorrow, gratitude, compassion, and zeal."[3]

Taking one of these, godly fear, Edwards points out that frequently in Scripture people "tremble at God's word, they fear before him, their flesh trembles because of him, they are afraid of his judgements, his excellency makes them afraid, and his dread falls upon them."[4]

Again and again he insists that affections are essential to spiritual life. A hard heart is an unaffected heart—a heart not moved by divine truth. "Hence the hard heart is called a stony heart, and is opposed to a heart of flesh, that has feeling and is sensibly touched and moved." His pastoral experience compelled him to conclude that nothing of religious significance ever took place in a human heart if it wasn't deeply affected by such godly emotions.[5]

Earlier I pointed out that feelings will result from our perception of spiritual realities. Volition and emotion are (in Edwards's view) parallel motions of the soul toward or away from something. Love and hate are thus bound up with those things we find ourselves reaching out for or avoiding.[6] Edwards asks, "Who will deny that true religion consists, in a great measure, in vigorous and lively actings of the *inclination* and *will* of the soul, or the fervent exercises of the heart?" And while he makes it clear that we are responsible for our emotions, in that our wills must be inclined to obedience and faith, he also makes it clear that the heart that knows little of them is in a sorry state.[7]

"In every act of the will *for* or *toward* something not present, the soul is in some degree *inclined* to that thing; and that inclination, if in a considerable degree, is the very same with the affection of *desire. . . . joy* or *delight*."[8]

Edwards claimed that feelings expressed the soul's movements. Without them a radical change of direction was not likely to follow. This explained why some people were never changed by the Word of God. "They hear . . . commands . . . warnings . . . and the sweet invitations of the gospel. Yet they remain as before . . . because they are not *affected* [moved] with what they hear."[9]

You can be so afraid of your feelings that you impair your capacity for truth. Scripture rings with the cries of people's hearts, their longings, their fears, their exultations and adorations. We begin to die the moment we refuse to feel. What we must fear is any carnal or evil source of our feelings, or any tendency to place our faith in our feelings rather than in God's Word.

The antithesis in Scripture is not between feelings and faith, but between sight (having to do with visible external reality) and faith. We say, "Seeing is believing," whereas Scripture teaches us we live by faith, not by sight (2 Cor 5:7). True, we should also love by faith rather than by feelings. But feelings commonly arise from faith—provided the faith is real. Thus while we must never be obsessed with feelings, we should sometimes be alerted by certain feelings or by the absence of others to the possibility that something is wrong.

Was Wesley wrong to record his subjective reactions on a certain famous May 24? "I went very unwillingly to a society in Aldersgate-Street, where one was reading Luther's preface to the Epistle to the Romans. About a quarter before nine, while he was describing the change which God works in the heart, I felt my heart strangely warmed. I felt I did trust in Christ, Christ alone for salvation: and an assurance was given me, that he had taken away my sins, even mine, and saved me from the law of sin and death."[10]

Wesley has been accused, and perhaps rightly, of too great a concern with his subjective states. But were those feelings of warmth, of trust and of assurance merely the psychological result of the reading, or were they the results of divine illumination, imparted by the Holy Spirit at that very moment?

Similar to the misunderstanding of the role of feelings in the role of the Christian life is that over the role of experience. It is possible to see a false antithesis between experience and what Scripture says. I sometimes hear people say, "Experience proves nothing." The statement is true, but usually it occurs when one side is interpreting Scripture in a way that does not jibe with the other side's experience. In such arguments either side could be in error. The experience might or might not be valid. The interpretation of Scripture could be correct or incorrect.

Recently I have been reading the writings of some of the great mystics. Many of them claimed to have revelations from God. Some such as Julian of Norwich (a fourteenth-century recluse) had almost no access to Scripture, yet her "showings" or revelations can reflect an accurate and profound knowledge of God and of salvation which many of us lack despite our knowledge of Scripture.

On the other hand, I find that several of the great mystics (such as Theresa of Avila, John of the Cross and the unknown author of *Cloud of Unknowing* to name only three) are alarmed at the readiness with which beginners in contemplative prayer claimed divine revelation as the source of their voices, dreams, visions and ecstatic bodily states. Apparently the Middle Ages abounded with people who were in love with their exotic experiences. In contrast, the real mystic was always keenly aware of how easy it is to be deceived both by one's deceitful heart, and by the subtlety of Satan.

As a psychiatrist I am ultracautious where the subjective is concerned, and most grateful for the firm ground for faith I have in Scripture. On the other hand, while it is good to affirm the authority of Scripture, none of us has a perfect grasp of it, and sometimes the understanding we have has never come alive in our daily walk, even though we have tried to trust and obey.

At times, too, our experience conflicts with what we thought Scripture said. At such times we should go back to Scripture to see whether in fact we had understood it correctly in the first place. We cannot always believe our eyes, our ears or our "spiritual experiences." But neither can we always trust our own or anyone else's exegesis. It is, therefore, helpful to have both exegesis and experience, each in its proper place.

There are twin dangers here, the dangers of reinterpreting Scripture in the light of experience, and the danger of forcing experience to conform with an incorrect notion of scriptural truth (that is, of denying reality in some way). All of us incline in one of these directions or in the other.

Opposite Dangers

And there is another point. We all have experience, whether we experience the supernatural or the total absence of the supernatural. And all of us tend to interpret Scripture according to the experience we have, whether it be negative or positive, present or absent. To deny the tendency is to deny our very humanity. Lloyd-Jones comments wryly on the matter:

Fanaticism . . . is a terrible danger which we must always bear in mind. It arises from a divorce between Scripture and experience, where we put experience above Scripture claiming things that are not sanctioned by Scripture, or are perhaps even prohibited by it.

But there is a second danger and it is equally important that we should bear it in mind. The second is the exact opposite of the first, as these things generally go from one violent extreme to the other. How difficult it always is to maintain a balance! The second danger, then, is that of being satisfied with something very much less than what is offered in the Scripture, and the danger of interpreting the Scripture by our experiences and reducing its teaching to the level of what we know and experience; and I would say that this second is the greater danger of the two at this present time.[11]

Here, surely, is the nub of the science/faith issue. Scientists observe (experience). All their observations turn out in the end to be based on personal experiences. Even scientific instruments that make "scientific" measurements have to be calibrated and read by our senses. Good scientists realize this and go to great lengths to check on their observations, subjecting them to many tests. When conflicts arise between science and faith/Scripture, the issues boil down to two—the same two that are involved with all issues of conflict involving Scripture and experience: (1) Are we dealing with scientific fact or scientific theory? And (2) are we dealing with biblical fact or biblical interpretation?

The height of folly is observable both among biblical scholars and Christians in the sciences. Some biblical scholars dismiss experience with contempt because they are so wedded to their own infallible understanding of Scripture. At the same time a minority of Christians in the sciences pursue their investigations with gleaming eyes and beating hearts, intent on defending the vulnerable Scripture with infallible scientific proofs. Personally I am repeatedly humbled as I discover how careful I must be. I jump to erroneous conclusions frequently, both when I read Scripture and when I am observing life around me. Bringing the two together has made me aware how poor I am at interpreting the one and observing and recording the other. Yet I move forward trusting that if anyone "lacks wisdom, he should ask God, who gives generously to all without finding fault, and it will be given to him" (Jas 1:5).

Recognizing Revival

Revival seems to cause no end of disagreements. One I haven't mentioned yet is theological disagreement. As my interest in revivals continued, I began to realize that there were two schools of thought about revival. One school emphasizes people and the other focuses on God. The first followed Charles Finney who told us we must repent. We had to plow the fallow ground of our hearts. According to the first school, revival comes when we implement God-ordained laws. The initiative lies in our own hands.

In contrast the second school saw revivals as sovereign acts of God. No amount of implementing laws will produce revival. God initiates the action. Only his effective call will awaken human repentance and obedience.

How important is the argument?

Whether we wait for it or work for it, the critical issue history raises is whether we will recognize it and embrace it when it comes.

Other questions are academic. Certainly there are not two kinds of revival, only an argument about how it works. Revival occurs both among Calvinists and Arminians. Right arguments and wrong arguments seem to make no difference as to who experiences it.

And while it is important to avoid gross heresy, I can only suppose that God does not allow our imperfect theologizings to impede his work. But failing to recognize his work can do harm. In the next two chapters, therefore, I will explore how we can discern whether or not revival and the manifestations that accompany it are the genuine article. If we can succeed here, we may be able to avoid the errors of so many in the past who reject true revival when it comes.

5

Are
Revival
Experiences
Psychological?

IN OUR EFFORT NOT TO REJECT TRUE RE-
vival but rather to discern if revival and its manifestations are of
God, we must ask a series of important questions: How should we
regard today's revival experiences? How can we explain them? Are
trembling, falling or whatever necessarily proof of the power of
God? Could revival follow? Or might the phenomena have a more
sinister explanation? On the other hand, should we categorize these
behaviors as merely psychological rather than supposing a supernatural cause?

The God of the Gaps?
Before addressing the meat of these questions, let me define some

terms. More than once I have used the word *supernatural*. To many
people the word implies that everything is divided into the Natural
and the Supernatural. There are things we can explain—that work
by themselves so to speak. They belong to the natural order or
Nature. And there is a mysterious Beyond which pokes its finger
into the here and now to produce a new wonder—or else to mess
things up. This we could call *Supernature*.

The Bible looks at things differently. Even the word *intervention*
may need careful examination. The finger of God is not a finger
poking from Supernature into Nature.

Most of us, you see, think of God as a "God of the gaps." We
don't intend to, but we do. Having been educated in the West there
is a deistic twist to our thinking, causing us to view a tree as
growing by natural laws. We fail to see God working everywhere
(God pulling and shaping each leaf, each blade of grass) even
though we may subscribe in general to the notion. We are affected
by our knowledge of science. Whatever our stated beliefs, in everyday practice we think of God setting the grass growing and then
moving off to do something else, so to speak.

The God of the Bible runs everything. He created Nature and
Supernature which are actually all of a piece with no division between them. Nothing in Nature works by itself. God "works" it.
He intervenes unceasingly. Every musical note we hear, every sunrise and sunset we see, every birth we rejoice in, every exploding
supernova we marvel at—all are expressions of his power. His
presence keeps the whole show working.

Similarly every angelic appearance, every miracle of healing are
likewise the working of his sovereign laws. In this sense there is no
fundamental difference between what we call miracle and what we
call ordinary. Yet we need some sort of a division to aid us in
discussion.

For instance, while there are some things science cannot explain
because science has not gone far enough, there are other things
science will never fathom. Some events do not belong to time and

space, which is the sphere to which the human mandate to govern is limited (and the only sphere in which science can therefore operate). Science cannot explain how the word of the Lord came to the prophets, for example, or how biblical prophecy works. Nor can science explain how Jesus walked on water. And because the unusual phenomena I write about are of the same order, I may from time to time use the term *supernatural*, without implying that science will one day explain the phenomena. I shall merely be talking about God intervening in what to us is an uncommon or unusual way. I shall not be implying that everything unusual or difficult to explain is the finger of God, but I shall insist that his finger does extraordinary things as well as ordinary ones as he acts in kindness and grace to men and women.

Let us settle the fact in our minds that certainly in Scripture, God's power may produce unusual reactions in human beings. Are such things happening today? Some people are said to tremble when the power of the Holy Spirit rests on them. Some weep or cry out. Others may shake violently and yet others fall to the ground. A few display bizarre bodily contortions.

We have already seen that this sort of behavior created problems in the days of Edwards, Whitefield and the Wesleys. It still does. Many of us feel uneasy in the presence of people who behave strangely. I am a psychiatrist, and even though I have spent years dealing with the bizarre and threatening behavior of psychotic patients, I still do not feel comfortable with it. Nor do I feel totally at ease when unusual behavior breaks out in church. But if God should be behind it, my personal reaction must be laid aside.

Assessing Manifestations

What then accounts for these strange behaviors? Logically the explanations could be of four types. We could suggest that—

1. People do it to themselves. That is to say, the manifestations have a psychological explanation, or are consciously or unconsciously self-induced.

2. Preachers do it to suggestible listeners—producing a so-called mass hysteria or mass hypnosis.

3. The devil does it—the phenomena representing some form of demonic control.

4. Or else God does it.

We have already been considering descriptions in Scripture of phenomena that result from the impact of the Spirit's power on fallen human beings. The Bible presents us with a world view in which causality cannot be limited to natural (matter and energy) forces. All events must be seen in terms of the interaction of visible and invisible elements. The question is not whether there is a supernatural explanation of a given event, for in all events—in everything that happens on earth—there is a supernatural explanation. The real question is: How do so-called Nature and Supernature combine in the event?

One of the four possibilities above must account for the behavioral phenomena seen in revival. For the theist the possibility must extend to two or three of the factors above in combination.

Of course we can never be sure of the extent to which we are in control of our own or anyone else's behavior. Alcohol-impaired drivers commonly believe they are in full control. On the other hand some people pretend not to be in control when they actually are.

In meetings where the power of the Holy Spirit is present, some manifestations are obviously not under the control of the affected individual. Others may behave suspiciously like an act. And sometimes a sensitive individual may say, "I had the feeling that I could 'break out' of what was happening to me."

To add to the complications, not only can strange behavior be self-induced consciously, but also unconsciously. That is, the behavior is psychological. And if the explanation is psychological it can be (1) a product of rigorous mental discipline; (2) a cheap attempt to gain attention or sympathy; or (3) an expression of an inner conflict the subject is unaware of.

Are Manifestations Self-Induced?

Let us start with mental discipline. You can learn to go into a trance state (a condition of altered consciousness) by following certain steps, steps that usually need to be practiced and may call for personal discipline. Christian as well as oriental mystics have for centuries described how you do it. Charles Tart has edited a book both examining the techniques and investigating the psychology of it.[1]

While some of the techniques are suspect, not all are evil. For instance some call for focusing attention for long periods on the person of God or on certain biblical truths. Mildly changed states of consciousness may result. Adepts may give themselves over to rigorous devotional exercises, so that in some sense they achieve the results. But the people whose behavior I shall describe later were not following steps or employing techniques, good or otherwise. In most cases they were taken by surprise. Therefore, I discount mental discipline as an explanation of what we are dealing with.

A second possibility is that the unusual behavior represents an attempt to draw attention to oneself, perhaps to gain sympathy. This happens frequently in times of revival and is not always dealt with sympathetically.

In meetings conducted by the Wesleys, powerful manifestations of the Spirit of God were frequent. Imitations also occurred. From Charles Wesley's journals, Dallimore has extracted the following passage:

> Some stumblingblocks, with the help of God, I have removed, particularly the fits. Many, no doubt, were, at our first preaching, struck down, both body and soul, into the depth of distress. Their outward affections were easy to be imitated. . . . Today, one . . . was pleased to fall into a fit for my entertainment, and beat himself heartily. I thought it a pity to hinder him; so . . . left him to recover at his leisure. Another girl, as she began to cry, I ordered to be carried out. Her convulsion was so violent,

as to take away the use of her limbs, till they laid and left her without the door. Then immediately she found her legs and walked off.[2]

I have spotted attention-seeking behavior in meetings where the power of the Holy Spirit is also manifest. Previous experience in psychiatry helped. I can understand and even sympathize with people giving way to it. Commonly inadequate and suffering from low self-esteem, such persons yearn for approval and love. They feel left out of the drama around them. They perceive, or think they perceive, that falling to the ground and trembling confer some sort of prestige. Some are fully aware of what they are doing. Others do not set out to deceive anyone unless it is that they deceive themselves. But they begin to believe that they too are about to fall. And they fall—or shake or moan or whatever.

Perhaps Charles Wesley's approach was right. It is better to ignore unobtrusive performances and to remove noisy ones. To give loving attention when it is sought in that particular way is to reinforce crazy behavior, and to make it more likely that the person will continue to "put on a performance" in order to gather a group of praying people around them. If love is to be shown, it is better shown at other times than as a reward for a demonstration.

Do They Come from Unconscious Urges?

But what about unconscious urges? Few of us are the masters of our bodies and emotions. Our behavior can embarrass and shame us. Psychoanalytic theories tell us we may be driven to behave a certain way because of fears, greeds and rages within us that we know nothing about. We have buried them deep within our beings, have forgotten them and are now blind and deaf to them. We may think we are fully in control of our actions, whereas we are prompted, at least in part, by unconscious drives.

The question then arises: Do people who shake and fall in religious meetings have an unconscious need to shake and fall? Do psychoanalytic theories explain the people Charles Wesley described as "struck down, both body and soul, into the depths of distress"? In an individual case it would be impossible to be sure. An unconscious urge is like a silent and invisible canary —you can neither prove nor disprove its presence. The critical questions will be: Why did the manifestation take the form it did at the time it did? What symbolic significance did the particular manifestation have? Why was the "unconscious material" released in those particular circumstances?

The question is important. "The heart is deceitful above all things and beyond cure. Who can understand it?" (Jer 17:9). God can and does. And when the power of his Spirit comes upon us what is hidden and latent may be awakened and stirred-up within us.

While unconscious conflicts may indeed influence the form of a manifestation I would say, not only on the basis of careful observation and history taking, but of my own personal experience, that the timing cannot be explained on such a hypothesis.

On Sunday, February 16, 1986, I listened to a man from Northern Ireland speak at the evening service of the Vineyard Fellowship in Anaheim. In a few brief sentences he described the dilemma there and expressed the hope that God would awaken and use the church in Northern Ireland to avert tragedy. We broke into groups for a brief time of prayer, after which John Wimber began the expository message for the evening. He had uttered only a few sentences when he paused and said, "I believe the Holy Spirit wants to share God's heart toward Northern Ireland with us." For a few moments there was silence. Then sounds of broken weeping could be heard all over the auditorium.

I watched and listened with a psychiatrist's interest. Suddenly, and greatly to my surprise, sobs began to rise from deep inside me. I suppressed them, and in my effort to do so my shoulders and chest began to shake. For a moment I was not certain what to think. Then I realized that I ought to stop being psychiatric and start to intercede for Ireland and for God's people there, and soon found myself (amid my stifled sobs) crying out silently to God for his mercy to that unhappy country.

Why did it happen to me just then? I am quite used to hearing people weep. I am also of an analytical turn of mind and somewhat overcontrolled, having a natural horror of letting my emotions be seen in public. I had not expected anything like this to happen to me. I was neither putting on a performance nor releasing unconscious urges. I believe my state represented a spirit of intercession stirred up by the Holy Ghost.

Dallimore gives a partly psychological explanation of the behavioral manifestations in John Wesley's meetings, contrasting them with those in Whitefield's (at which large numbers of people were more inclined to weep silently). "The reason for this difference probably lies in the fact that, in the preaching of Harris, Charles Wesley and Whitefield, emotion was freely expressed, while in that of John Wesley it was largely pent up. . . . Such was his self-control that in preaching he usually remained outwardly placid. His hearers, however, though they found a terrible sense of guilt arising within them, seemed to find themselves forbidden by the preacher's self-command to express their feelings in any way, till these at last burst forth with violence."[3]

Dallimore could be right, but I am inclined to doubt it. Even when he was not preaching to Wesley's people, Whitefield on at least two occasions experienced some of the same manifestations as Wesley (we shall look at some of these later). In any case does placid preaching, whatever its content, commonly induce "a terrible sense of guilt"? Dynamic and volatile preaching is more likely to do so. Any restraint imposed by Wesley's manner would be more likely to result in a greater explosion of weeping or fearful trembling (when distress had passed the point of control) than in bizarre behavior.

Are Manifestations Preacher-Induced?
In *The Golden Cow* I described brainwashing techniques that can be

used to change people's beliefs and modify their behavior.[4] In *Flirting with the World* I also warned of the dangers of certain counseling trends in the seventies and eighties.[5] New Age advocates tell us to seek experiences that will expand our consciousness, enabling us to enter a new stage of being. Once sought through mind-expanding drugs (as people like Timothy Leary and Aldous Huxley urged) these states are now produced by techniques such as est (Ehrhardt Seminars Training) and more recently Forum. Douglas Groothuis describes a typical session.

In the est experience several hundred people are brought together for two successive weekends of marathon sessions designed to help them get "it." During the sessions they are confined to their chairs for long hours without note-taking, talking, smoking, clock-watching or sitting next to anyone they know. Minimal food and bathroom breaks are strictly observed. Each of the sixteen hour sessions is led by a trainer who berates, taunts and humiliates the crowd by insisting that their lives don't work. The sustained intensity leads many to become sick, cry or break down in some other way. That's the goal. Through the agonizing hours of torture the tears turn to insight and the sickness into enlightenment. The participants are told, "You're part of every atom in the world and every atom is part of you. We are all gods who created our own worlds." Eventually the people—at least some of them—claim to get "it"; they experience enlightenment and oneness.[6]

The Ehrhardt technique, quite apart from the sinister teaching which is pantheistic and monistic, is similar to the brainwashing techniques used in student meetings in communist China following the revolution. It is "preacher-manipulation" par excellence.

Brainwashing techniques major on the following elements: (1) physical exhaustion; (2) changes in perceptual levels; (3) cognitive dissonance; (4) inducing a sense of guilt and/or inadequacy and failure; (5) inducing fear; (6) inducing a sense of hopelessness; and (7) crowd effect.

Let me explain what I mean by changes in perceptual levels. All of us are accustomed to a certain level of perceptual input. Day and night our bodies are bombarded continuously by sights, sounds sensations and smells. We get used to certain levels of this ongoing bombardment. We not only tolerate it, we grow uneasy when it stops. Too much or too little makes us anxious. And anxiety, when it reaches intolerable levels, can lead to withdrawal, to rage and to uncontrolled behavior.

Take noise, for example. Adolescents who like rock music grow accustomed to loud sounds that many older people find hard to tolerate. It is the volume of the sound that becomes the bone of contention, for it is the volume that determines levels of relaxation and of anxiety. Once they have grown accustomed to it, younger people "need" the same input of sound if they are to experience relaxation. Lower levels leave them restless, mildly anxious. But the levels that relax adolescents disturb anyone who has never become accustomed to them, raising their anxiety levels.

So if you want to manipulate people, work on their input levels. Scream the gospel at them for a while. Then to keep them off balance switch to a quiet, intimate joke or two. Then start shrieking again. Your audience will soon get a high anxiety level and be putty in your hands.

Cognitive dissonance has to do with our expectations, and to some extent with our hopes and fears. We expect the earth to feel solid beneath us. We do not anticipate that when we stand on it that it will weave and shake beneath our feet. Terror arises in an earthquake because of the incongruity between what our lifelong daily experience has taught us (that the walls and the ground are solid) and the new reality of a heaving earth and billowing walls.

To manipulate a large number of people you need to exhaust them, to bombard them with levels of sensation they are not accustomed to, to expose them to concepts that frighten them, to humiliate them and make them feel guilty and hopeless, while still offering a new and magical idea. Crowd effect will be on your side, in that the crowd tends to carry individuals along with it. Writes Dr. Louis Linn, "Students of mob psychology have observed the elation, the impulsivity, the general emotional regression, and the personality dissociation that can occur in seemingly normal adults when they become part of a mob."[7]

Could brainwashing explain what happened in Edwards's meetings? in Wesley's? in Whitefield's? What about contemporary teachers such as John Wimber? I would say it is unlikely. In the Vineyard meetings and seminars, where the teaching is to my mind biblical, I have noted that people are encouraged to feel free to use bathroom facilities, that breaks to stretch and chat or to have coffee are frequent, and that while the preaching can at times be intense, it is more usually low key. Crowd effect and preaching technique could not account for the onset of the manifestations, though crowd effect might cause some people to "join in the fun."

Examples of manipulative preaching are not, however, hard to find. Such preaching can and does stir up emotion, and under it both spurious and real decisions are made. But the kind of behavior we are talking about does not occur unless the Holy Spirit has originally started the ball rolling. But while I feel that Wesley, Whitefield and certainly Edwards can be exonerated from the charge of manipulation, other preachers cannot. Many early nineteenth-century preachers opened themselves to charges of bad management and extreme emotional pressure. In their meetings behavioral manifestations occurred, along with flagrantly sinful behavior. Even so, I doubt that they were responsible for all the behavioral manifestations.

Charles A. Johnson describes the camp meetings that took place in open fields at the end of the eighteenth and during the early nineteenth centuries as the frontiers advanced westward across North America. Violence, gambling, robbery, drunkenness and sexual immorality were common in the open societies the advancing frontier created. Preachers sent by God to reach them used colorful language to describe the terrors of hell and the glories of heaven. Among their congregations would be drunken, ribald scoffers. And from all the camp meetings come reports of many conversions and of the kind of manifestations we are talking about.

Johnson accuses the preachers of extreme emotionalism and by their language of deliberately arousing fear.[8] He describes unusual noise levels in exhausting meetings which commonly continued until dawn.

Perhaps the most famous of the camp meetings took place in Cane Ridge, Kentucky, when between ten and twenty-five thousand people gathered from August 6-12, 1801. The meetings continued without intermission by day through rain and sunshine, and at night by torch and firelight. The organizer and most of the preachers seem to have been Presbyterian, but every shade of opinion apparently was represented. Several preachers might have been seen preaching simultaneously from different makeshift pulpits. People slept on the ground as the need for rest overcame them.

Johnson describes it as "in all probability, the most disorderly, the most hysterical, and the largest" of such efforts to be held in early America. Cited by critics as typical of revival in general, Johnson points out that the meetings were in fact highly atypical. Alcoholics brought their liquor with them, and drunkenness and sexual promiscuity were not uncommon. One lady of easy virtue set herself up under a preaching stand, until she was discovered there with her male consorts. And the spontaneous excitement created by so unusual an event probably contributed to unguarded conduct in some people.

The association of these and many other manifestations with drunken and immoral conduct leaves a sour taste in our mouths. We instinctively feel that everything at the camp meeting must have been tarred with the same evil brush. On the other hand a God of mercy seems to have looked down on the meeting, and visited it in compassion and with power. Many people were afflicted with the "falling exercise," presumably what is now called "being slain in the spirit." (At one point a conscientious Presbyterian minister carefully counted three thousand fallen people.) Other people of all ages and social classes sometimes lay writhing on the ground, weeping, crying out to God for mercy.

Johnson quotes the impressions of James B. Finley, who was at the time a free thinker.

> The noise was like the roar of Niagara. The vast sea of human beings seemed to be agitated as if by a storm. . . . Some of the people were singing, others praying, some crying for mercy in the most piteous accents, while others were shouting vociferously. While witnessing these scenes, a peculiarly-strange sensation, such as I had never felt before, came over me. My heart beat tumultuously, my knees trembled, my lip quivered, and I felt as though I must fall to the ground. A strange supernatural power seemed to pervade the entire mass of mind there collected. . . . Soon after I left and went into the woods, and there I strove to rally and man up my courage.
>
> After some time I returned to the scene of excitement, the waves of which, if possible, had risen still higher. The same awfulness of feeling came over me. I stepped up on to a log, where I could have a better view of the surging sea of humanity. The scene that then presented itself to my mind was indescribable. At one time I saw at least five hundred, swept down in a moment as if a battery of a thousand guns had been opened upon them, and then immediately followed shrieks and shouts that rent the very heavens. . . . I fled for the woods a second time, and wished I had stayed at home.[9]

Finley's reaction to what he saw is interesting. He had gone to the meetings as a "freethinking" observer, a role which would provide a good deal of protection from manipulation and crowd effect, unless something else made him feel threatened. Even in a disorderly, ill-run meeting where manipulative preaching may have abounded, the grace and the power of God does not seem to have been absent.

To decide if all revival phenomena are the result of manipulation, we will have to examine the preaching under which those phenomena occurred. But the fact is that both in Scripture and in church history godly preachers, far from being manipulative, have sought to suppress manifestations, which sometimes persist in spite of the preacher's attempts to stop them.

We have already looked at the revival that broke out during the fifth century B.C. in Jerusalem. Confronted by a mass reaction of distressed weeping as the Holy Spirit moved on postexilic Jews, Nehemiah, Ezra and the Levites did all they could to calm the people. They cried, "This day is sacred to the LORD your God. Do not mourn or weep. . . . Go and enjoy choice food and sweet drinks, and send some to those who have nothing prepared. . . . Do not grieve, for the joy of the LORD is your strength" (Neh 8:9-10).

We saw before that the instruction preceding the outbreak was far from manipulative (Neh 8:1-8). The weeping could be attributed only to the Holy Spirit's activity in creating a hunger for truth and in making the people aware of how far they had departed from it. And the reality of the work became evident as a series of godly reforms followed the revival (Neh 9—10).

Henry Venn gives an interesting account of Whitefield's preaching in a parish churchyard in 1757.

Under Mr. Whitefield's sermon, many of the immense crowd that filled every part of the burial ground, were overcome with fainting. Some sobbed deeply; others wept silently . . . when he came to impress the injunction in the text . . . several of the congregation burst into the most piercing bitter cries. Mr. Whitefield, at this juncture, made a pause and then burst into a flood of tears.

During this short interval Mr. Madan and myself stood up, and requested people to restrain themselves as much as possible, from making any noise. Twice afterwards we had to repeat the same counsel. . . . When the sermon was ended people seemed chained to the ground. [We] found ample employment in en-

deavouring to comfort those broken down under a sense of
guilt.[10]

We may conclude that Whitefield was emotionally moved on this
occasion, but we may not conclude that he was manipulative. Manipulation demands control of oneself and of the situation. The
manipulator may act emotional (manipulate his own emotions) but
it will be with an innate grasp of the total situation. Underneath,
the manipulator is coldly using his or her emotions to achieve an
effect. This is not what Whitefield was doing.

And the intervention of Venn and Madan was identical to the
intervention of Ezra and Nehemiah in the revival of Nehemiah 8.
Clearly there was no attempt to foster or to prolong the fainting
spells or an emotional outbreak.

I described earlier how several thousand people were powerfully
moved to intercede for Northern Ireland in the evening service at
the Vineyard Christian Fellowship, many with bitter tears. As they
wept and prayed John Wimber made no attempt to milk the situation but remained silent for several minutes. Then he prayed,
"Now, Lord, grant your servants a spirit of peace!" In less than a
minute the weeping had ceased, and without further comment
Wimber proceeded with his exposition. Neither the weeping nor
the cessation of the weeping had been preacher-produced. Wimber
had made no mention of weeping and remained silent throughout
it. God had briefly shared his heart with his people.

Certainly there are dangers associated with the manifestations we
are talking about, and we shall take a closer look at them in a later
chapter. In the next chapter, however, we must continue to consider the possibility that even today they may result from spiritual
power, whether diabolical or godly.

6
Are Revival Experiences Spiritual?

ONCE WHEN I WAS TRAVELING IN SOUTHern Brazil, I saw a great shaft of rock rising hundreds of feet into the sky. "What do they call it?" I asked my Brazilian companion.

"They call it the Finger of God," he replied.

I had no idea then that the expression came from the book of Exodus. Confronted by the sight of God's power through Aaron's rod, Egyptian magicians assumed that Aaron's source of power was similar to their own. In fact they demonstrated as much by reproducing Aaron's ability to transform a rod into a serpent, then by turning water into blood and eventually by conjuring up frogs from

Egypt's dust, they found they had met their match. Suddenly they discovered they had been mistaken. Unable to succeed in imitating Moses and Aaron, they went to Pharaoh and said, "This is the finger of God" (Ex 8:19).

The phrase is a metaphor, an anthropomorphic metaphor if you like. It is a colorful way of referring to the awesome nature of divine power, and it carries with it the reminder that it is unwise to look at what God does and to lightly conclude that another power is responsible.

So far I have tried to answer the questions: Do people produce manifestations themselves? And, do preachers produce them by manipulating people? With the cautions of the Exodus story clearly in mind, let us now ask whether demons produce the physical manifestations found in revivals.

When Hell's Gates Start to Rattle

Many Christians shake their heads in alarm at the notion that the Spirit's presence might cause demons to act up. The idea seems incongruous. They feel the Spirit would cause demons to sneak away in silence and shame. Scripture and history both teach us the opposite. When the Spirit is present in power, demons may flee, but they protest and make their presence known. Their power and kingdom are exposed and menaced.

Following his triumph over temptation, Jesus was ministering in the authority and power of the Holy Spirit when one demon in terror cried out, "Ha! What do you want with us, Jesus of Nazareth? Have you come to destroy us? I know who you are—the Holy One of God!" (Lk 4:34). Other demons cried, "You are the Son of God!" (Lk 4:41). The presence of Jesus provoked demonic outcries.

Even Satanic delusions, wrong ideas that creep in to spoil a work of God, far from being an indication that the work itself is Satanic, may in fact serve as a proof of the very opposite. Jonathan Edwards wisely comments, "Nor are . . . delusions of Satan intermixed with the work, any argument that the work in general is not of the Spirit of God."[1] Wherever the Spirit moves powerfully, an enemy not only opposes but seeks to undermine.

John Wesley was not surprised when demons manifested themselves in Christian gatherings. In public and in private he found himself contending with them.[2] John Cennick, one of his preacher-associates, tells us:

> One night more than twenty roared and shrieked together while I was preaching . . . [some of whom] confessed they were demoniacs. Sally Jones could not read and yet would answer if persons talked to her in Latin or Greek. They could tell who was coming into the house, who would be seized next, what was doing in other places, etc. . . .
>
> I have seen people so foam and violently agitated that six men could not hold one, but he would spring out of their arms or off the ground, and tear himself, as in hellish agonies. Others I have seen sweat uncommonly, and their necks and tongues swell and twist out of all shape. Some prophesied and some uttered the worst of blasphemies against our Saviour.[3]

In areas where witchcraft is practiced overtly, open conflict between the kingdom of God and the rule of darkness is common. Wherever the power of the king is displayed and his glorious banners allowed to stream, the powers of darkness may tremble, but they resist. Demonic manifestations are common and may be physically dangerous.

In chapter one we met Carlos Annacondia, the pentecostal evangelist from Argentina who escaped an assassination attempt during one of his *conquistas*. Annacondia is often criticized for paying too much attention to the devil and his minions. On a recent visit to Argentina I asked Annacondia about this emphasis. He told me he does not always rebuke the devil publicly. Rather he only does so when he feels the Holy Spirit leads him to. Annacondia maintains that the various cults and witches that organize attempts to break up his meetings are driven by demonic forces. They presence themselves in the meetings, especially in the earlier stages of a given evangelistic campaign. He will speak against them until the back of the local spiritual opposition has been broken.

Ralph Humphries, an associate of the Wesleys and Whitefield, put it this way: "I think the case was often this; the word of God would come with convincing light and power into the hearts and consciences of sinners, whereby they were so far awakened. . . . [that] the peace of the strong man armed would be disturbed; hell within would begin to roar; the devil, that before, being unmolested, lay quiet in their hearts, would now be stirred up."[4]

My own experiences over the past three years confirm this view. However, I must add that only a minority of the manifestations I have observed have been demonic. And when they have occurred, unless the demonic presences can be dismissed immediately, those in charge of ministry teams have usually seen to it that the victims are quietly taken somewhere so they can receive ministry privately, without being exposed to embarrassment.

But how do we distinguish what is of God from what is of Satan?

Over the long haul there is no problem in making the distinction between something that reflects a demonic presence from something that does not. In any case, experience over at least the past three hundred years seems to indicate that here in the West the overwhelming majority of manifestations have not been demonic. The difficulty arises in an immediate situation. How do we decide on the spot what is happening? Experience may be helpful, but if you have no experience, what then?

To begin, we should rid ourselves of two great enemies of discernment—idle curiosity and fear. Idle curiosity has no place in the battle with the powers of darkness. As for fear, it is not only inappropriate, it hinders discernment. It is inappropriate because demons have been around a long time and have probably been also affecting the person in whom the manifestation is occurring for a long time. A solution should be sought, but there is no urgency about solving the matter in the next ten seconds.

Fear impedes discernment since learning to distinguish the spirits grows in the soil of quiet confidence in God the Holy Spirit. The more relaxed and at peace we are in the Lord, the more easily will we discern what is demonic. If we are inexperienced, it is wise to seek the help of someone who is experienced.

There are some particular indications of demonic manifestations that will be discussed in more detail in subsequent chapters. Usually when they occur in Christian settings they include such things as blasphemous utterances, voices other than the person's own voice coming from the throat of an individual, animal-like movements and gestures (such as snakelike writhing).

Manifestations Produced by the Holy Spirit

The Holy Spirit produced most of the manifestations we shall be discussing. Many people had no means of anticipating what was going to happen to them. Some (like Saul of Tarsus) were vigorously opposed, feeling it was all fraudulent.

If we doubt the genuineness of the whole thing we should consider several factors. First, we must examine the teaching under which the manifestations occur (not relying only on gossipy reports since in every revival, critics distort the content of the preaching). Then we must observe the results in the lives of the people in whom they occur. Finally, we must not forget the element of surprise. People with no previous knowledge of what might happen, who were under no kind of stress, others of whom were resisting what they saw happening around them—all have been affected.

For instance, my wife and I had unconsciously always entertained a stereotypical idea of what it would be like when the Spirit came with power. The reality differed from our unconscious stereotype. During a quiet lecture given at Fuller in 1985 neither of us knew the Spirit was powerfully present. And certainly neither of us suspected that she would tremble at such a time.

At first Lorrie was puzzled and embarrassed at her shaking. She tried to hide the marked tremor in her hands and arms (a tremor that continued to recur periodically for several weeks). Having observed what was happening to Lorrie, I turned to view the rest of the class (mainly of missionaries and noncharismatic pastors). From my front row seat I saw several people in a similar predicament to hers. Some of them seemed dazed but at peace. The power of God's Spirit could evidently affect people physically even during a quiet lecture period.

It also occurs in people who not only do not believe in such things but who firmly oppose them. In a journal entry dated May 1, 1769, John Wesley records the bewilderment of an indignant Quaker who was disgusted by the manifestations he saw in one of Wesley's meetings: "A quaker, who stood by, was not a little displeased at the dissimulation of these creatures and was biting his lips and knitting his brows, when he dropped down as thunderstruck. The agony he was in was even terrible to behold. We besought God not to lay folly to his charge. And he soon lifted up his head and cried aloud, 'Now I know thou art a prophet of the Lord!' "[5]

Wesley records an even more dramatic instance in a man who witnessed the above incident and who had spent several days warning people about the errors of Wesley and the danger of what was happening in his meetings. He records the incident in a letter to his brother Samuel, dated May 10, 1739.

A bystander, one John Haydon, was quite enraged at this, and, being unable to deny something supernatural in it, laboured beyond all measure to convince all his acquaintance, that it was a delusion of the devil.

I was met in the street the next day by one who informed me that John Haydon was fallen raving mad. It seems he had sat down to dinner, but wanted first to make an end to a sermon he was reading. At the last page he suddenly changed colour, fell off his chair, and began screaming terribly, beating himself against the ground.

I found him on the floor, the room being full of people, whom his wife would have kept away; but he cried out, "No; let them all come; let all the world see the judgement of God."

Two or three were holding him as well as they could. He immediately fixed his eyes on me, and said, "Aye, this is he I said deceived the people; but God hath overtaken me. I said it was a delusion of the devil; but this is no delusion."

Then he roared aloud, "O thou devil! Thou cursed devil! Yea, thou legion of devils! Thou canst not stay in me. Christ will cast thee out. I know his work is begun. Tear me to pieces if thou wilt. But thou canst not hurt me."

He then beat himself again, and groaned again, with violent sweats, and heaving of the breast. We prayed with him, and God put a new song in his mouth. The words were, which he pronounced with a clear, strong voice, "This is the Lord's doing, and it is marvelous in our eyes. This is the day which the Lord hath made: We will rejoice and be glad in it. Blessed be the Lord God of Israel, from this time forth for evermore."[6]

It is foolish to suggest that such opponents of the Great Awakening had secret wishes to be convinced. People of this sort have more in common with Saul of Tarsus on the Damascus road, or with the brief incident in John 18:6, where at Christ's majestic confession, "I am he," his captors fell backward to the ground. (John's meaning is clear. The fall had no natural explanation. In the presence of the I AM, the rabble were knocked down by the power of God.)

Similar incidents occur from time to time in the ministry of John Wimber, the most recent being in Sheffield, England, on November 6, 1985. A pastor who had been invited by a colleague decided with some reluctance to attend. He arrived late, entering the building at a point when Wimber was inviting the Holy Spirit to take charge. Disgusted, his worst fears realized, he turned to leave in protest. But before he could reach the door he was struck down shaking and was unable to rise for a prolonged period. Eventually he left the building a profoundly changed man.

At the same meeting was David White. Afterward he wrote the

following letter to John Wimber in which he describes his experience at the meeting in full.

Dear John:

Excuse my familiarity, but I feel I know you personally. . . . I went to Sheffield (having previously worshipped at David Pytches' Church in Chorley Wood), and I feel God has given me a totally new ministry, and a fresh start. And it was badly needed. I work and live in Toxteth, just about one of the worst areas in Liverpool, and at times I have got so discouraged. But since Sheffield my life has undergone a dramatic change.

This is really why I am writing; please, please could you tell me what exactly you proclaimed in your blessing on the Thursday night at Sheffield!

I heard about the first three sentences and then POW!! It was incredible. God fell on me, I was utterly broken, my whole life lay before him on the line. I thought he was going to kill me—so much so, I said goodbye to my wife Ruth. It was awesome, and painful, as what felt like high voltage electricity burned through me.

Friends around me described it like I was being stretched. There appeared to be a force around me. And this lasted about fifteen minutes, and then I thought I had died because my body seemed filled, transparent with light. Then, "That's nice—the angels know 'our God reigns'!!" It seems to me that there is a connection between what you prayed for the pastors and my experience. And I want to know. Since then God has confirmed that experience with similar anointings—what is God wanting to do with me?

I hope you don't mind me writing. Be assured of my prayers and please pray that I may remain humble and close to the Lord. And may the Lord protect you and yours.

Yours, in much thankfulness in our lovely Lord,
David White

To theorize that these men were unconsciously desiring such an experience may be an interesting intellectual exercise. Certainly the first man consciously wished the very opposite. But even if they were, the Holy Spirit was the one whose power and grace brought their unconscious wish to the surface.

About a year after the Sheffield conference I received permission from David White to publish his letter. Some of his comments are interesting. "I would not wish any to think they have to copy my experience," he wrote, "nor would I wish anyone to make unwarranted conclusions about how 'spiritual' a person I am. . . . Of course, the letter has about it the air of new, fresh enthusiasm— that 'POW' makes me cringe now! Yet it is an accurate and valid description."

But what benefits had accrued to him? "Sheffield marked a turning point in my life. In terms of subsequent growth and usefulness to the Lord it has been one of the most significant experiences since conversion. . . . In my ministry I have a new found authority and a greater expectancy of God to work than ever before." He commented on Lloyd-Jones's book *Joy Unspeakable*, and wondered how to categorize his experience. "In one sense, what to call the experience theologically does not bother me, as long as I do not make extravagant claims for perfection and thus repeat the mistakes made in church history. . . ."

For my part I am glad that God ignores our petty notions of propriety as he deals with men and women. I want God to be God. But because I suffer from a skeptical disposition I have to see for myself what is happening, to inquire, to test. For though I want to see God acting as God, I have no wish to find anything less. David White's testimony speaks for itself.

Having therefore seen and examined carefully, I am convinced that while some manifestations represent psychological aberrations, and others demonic fear and protest, many and perhaps most of the manifestations evidence the presence in power of the Holy Spirit. But these manifestations, while they may be a blessing, are no guarantee of anything. Their outcome depends on the mysterious traffic between God and our spirits. Your fall and your shaking may be a genuine expression of the power of the Spirit resting on you. But the Spirit may not benefit you in the least if God does not have his way with you, while someone who neither trembles nor falls may profit greatly.

The Orchards and the Fruit

Surely it is fruit that matters. And specific fruits tend to be found in certain kinds of orchards. Earlier I pointed out that by their very nature, dramatic behavioral manifestations arouse strong feelings in onlookers. Critics turn away in disgust. Enthusiasts praise the Lord and long for more. And both may suffer from a wrong way of looking at matters. Each evaluates the manifestations by the wrong criteria, assuming a different, but too simple explanation. In itself, a given manifestation is no sign that something of spiritual value has been accomplished.

According to Edwards, neither a negative nor a positive judgment should be based on the manifestation alone "because the Scripture nowhere gives us any such rule."[7] How then is a manifestation to be judged? Partly by the orchard—the setting the manifestation occurs in, the kind of preaching the subject has listened to. And partly by the fruit—effects on the life, the ongoing testimony and the subsequent character of the person in whom the manifestation is observed.

Edwards devotes a good deal of attention to what I have called the orchard, focusing mainly on the kind of preaching under which the manifestations occur. In a paper entitled "The Distinguishing Marks of a Work of the Spirit of God"[8] he expounds 1 John 4:1, "Dear friends, do not believe every spirit, but test the spirits to see whether they are from God, because many false prophets have gone out into the world."

He asks the question: How can one spot a genuine, as distinct from a false, prophet? And in expounding the whole of 1 Jn 4 he answers: by noting whether his preaching affirms the historic Jesus as the crucified and risen Messiah; whether it opposes sin and worldly lust; whether it awakens respect for Scripture by affirming its truth and its divine source; whether it awakens an awareness of the shortness of life and the coming of judgment; and finally, whether it awakens genuine love both toward God and one's neighbor.

But the fruit is more important than the orchard. An enemy can plant evil trees in the best regulated orchard. "By their fruit," Jesus tells us, "you will recognize them. Do people pick grapes from thornbushes, or figs from thistles?" (Mt 7:16). Because fruit is so important I have devoted the second section of this book to biographical accounts of people I have interviewed in whom manifestations have occurred.

But it is time that we looked in more detail at specific examples of the manifestations we are talking about.

7
Varieties of Revival Experiences

T RUE RELIGION, IN GREAT PART CONSISTS *in holy affections."* JONATHAN EDWARDS
"Restrained! Quiet! Unobtrusive! My dear friends, why not listen to the evidence? This is the kind of thing that happens when the Spirit 'comes' upon man, even the building was shaken. . . ." D. MARTYN LLOYD-JONES

If you read the history of revivals conscientiously, you will read about some pretty unusual behavior in revival meetings. The behaviors we shall examine here are the commoner varieties of the late twentieth century, displayed by people whose background is either pagan or conservatively Christian. Of these the easiest to understand are expressions of emotion.

Let us begin then by looking at three manifestations of emo-tion—those of fear, of sorrow and of joy.

Terror and the Numinous

In Scripture there seem to be two different types of fear of God. There is the fear of the disobedient servant, and there is also what has been called *numinous fear*.

Moses experienced both kinds on different occasions. In Exodus 4:24-26 there is a disturbing account of the first kind of fear—the fear of the disobedient servant. Moses and Zipporah are on their way to Egypt with their family. Moses' firstborn son is uncircum-cised. In a single shattering sentence we learn that "at a lodging place on the way, the LORD met Moses and was about to kill him." Only after Zipporah carried out the circumcision, smearing the blood on Moses' foot, did the danger pass.

The incident is as rare as it is disturbing and mysterious. Two conditions seem to be of importance. First, Moses is a servant chosen for a special mission for which absolute obedience and devotedness to God and his word are essential, and second, Moses' attitude has been ambivalent. He has been playing fast and loose with the divine covenant. He has been reluctant, perhaps because of Zipporah's obvious distaste for the custom, to circumcise his son. And in a servant whose role is to be crucial, his ambivalence is not to be tolerated.

During the past two years I have come across two episodes of such a terror—the terror of persons who, caught up in a mystical experience, thought that God was about to kill them. Both inci-dents took place when the subjects were fully awake and out-of-doors at night. Both people were also servants of God who were about to back away from his call on their lives. In terror they both instantly repented.

We shrink from the concept of God this suggests to us. But that is because we have no real understanding of his burning rage against all sin.

But commoner and more understandable than the fear Moses and Zipporah experienced is the fear felt by finite, sinful men and women in the presence of an infinite and holy God. The reactions of Daniel and John the apostle that I mentioned earlier are such cases.

Dr. Rudolph Otto, theologian and philosopher, in his book, *The Idea of the Holy* writes about the " 'supra rational' in the depths of the divine nature." God's holiness is ultimate moral beauty, moral beauty of such a nature and such power that it transcends human understanding. It is the living God himself. He can, and at times he actually does, communicate it—and himself—to us. As Thomas Binney wrote:

Eternal Light! Eternal Light!
How pure the soul must be
When placed within Thy searching sight,
It shrinks not, but with calm delight
Can live, and look on Thee!

Oh, how shall I, whose native sphere
Is dark, whose mind is dim,
Before th'Ineffable appear,
And on my naked spirit, bear
The uncreated beam?

According to Otto a number of elements can be distinguished in men and women who have thus encountered God. He vigorously denies Schleiermacher's assertion that these elements are mere extensions of those feelings devout Jews and Christians experience in their worship, feelings of awe and reverence, even of rapture, seeing these at best as analogies of one to whom God has revealed himself in a close encounter.[1]

Otto uses, as C. S. Lewis did later, the term *numinous* to describe this quality of the fear. The numinous experience is made up of an overwhelming sense of one's creaturehood, such that one experiences a "submergence into nothingness before an overpowering absolute might."[2] Other elements are what he calls, *Mysterium Tremendum* which is not "that which is hidden and esoteric, [but] that which is beyond conceptual understanding, extraordinary and unfamiliar."[3]

The fear may be mingled with joy, so that people are overcome with wonder and adoration, and like Rat in *The Wind in the Willows* they say, "Afraid? Of Him? Oh, never! And yet . . . I am afraid."

For Jonathan Edwards the fear was crucial. "The Scriptures place much of religion in godly fear; insomuch that an experience of it is often spoken of as the character of those who are truly religious persons. They tremble at God's word, they fear before him, their flesh trembles because of him, they are afraid of his judgments, his excellency makes them afraid, and his dread falls upon them."[4]

Whether people's fear is fear of God's judgment on sin, or of the ineffability of his person, Christians and non-Christians alike experience his fear during times of revival. In Cambuslang, Scotland, in 1742, Dr. Alexander Webster described meetings there: "Many cry out in the bitterness of their soul. Some . . . from the stoutest men to the tenderest child, shake and tremble and a few fall down as dead. Nor does this only happen when men of warm address alarm them with the terrors of the law, but when the most deliberate preacher speaks of redeeming love. . . ."[5]

I have felt such a fear. I have trembled, perspired, known my muscles turn to water. On one occasion it was as I prayed with elders and deacons in my home. I had tried to teach them what worship was, but I doubt that on that occasion they understood. We then turned to prayer. Perhaps partly to be a model to them I began to express worship, conscious of the poverty of my words. Then suddenly I saw in front of me a column of flame of about two feet in width. It seemed to arise from beneath the floor and to pass through the ceiling of the room. I knew—without being told—knew by some infallible kind of knowing that transcended the use of my intellect, that I was in the presence of the God of holiness. In stunned amazement I watched a rising column of flames in our own living room, while my brothers remained with their heads quietly bowed and their eyes closed.

Did they know what was happening? They made no comment afterward and I never asked them. In some obscure fashion I felt I was in the presence of reality and that my brothers were asleep. For years afterward I never spoke of the incident. The others who were present could not have perceived the blend of stark terror and joy that threatened to sweep me away. How could I live and see what I saw? Garbled words of love and of worship tumbled out of my mouth as I struggled to hang on to my self-control. I was no longer trying to worship. Worship was undoing me, pulling me apart. And to be pulled apart was both terrifying and full of glory.

Grief and Mourning

Strong emotions are rarely pure. They come (depending on how clearly we see truth) in twos and threes, in jumbled and incongruous liaisons. Fear may be coupled with grief, joy with fear, rage with pity. "The town seemed to be full of the presence of God; it was never so full of love, nor of joy, and yet so full of distress, as it was then."[6] writes Jonathan Edwards of the 1735 revival in New Hampshire.

Edwards uses the term *melting* when in his journal he describes weeping that took place on Saturday, March 1, 1746, in a catechism class he held in Crossweeksung, New Jersey: "Toward the close of my discourse, divine truths made considerable impressions upon the audience, and produced tears and sobs in some under concern; and more especially a sweet and humble melting in sundry that, I have reason to hope, were truly gracious."[7]

Dr. John Hamilton, in a similar vein, gives his own description of the revival in Cambuslang, Scotland: "I found a good many persons under the deepest exercise of soul, crying out most bitterly of their lost and miserable state, by reason of sin; of their unbelief, in despising Christ and the offers of the Gospel; . . . I heard them express great sorrow for these things, and seemingly in the most serious and sincere manner, and this not so much . . . from fear of punishment as from a sense of the dishonour done to God. . . ."[8]

Two occasions of such weeping in John Wimber's meetings stand out in my memory. In March 1984, in the Vineyard church in Anaheim, Wimber invited the unsaved to come forward for counsel and prayer. His address had been restrained, certainly not emotional. I estimate that about two hundred people instantly began to move to the front of the church without any pressure. Many burst into tears as they did so, some stopping on their way to the front and turning to anyone near them with an agonized and totally unsolicited outpouring of confession of sin.

A second manifestation of sorrow over sin took place in a seminar in Vancouver eighteen months later. Wimber had spoken of pastors who in the face of critical scholarship had watered down the biblical content of their preaching, thus robbing the sheep of truth. He then invited any pastors who felt convicted by God of such sin, and who wished to renounce it and preach the truth, to come forward for prayer. A large number responded. Some of these spontaneously began to weep. I stood very close to the group and estimated that about one in seven was affected in this way.

Joy Unspeakable

Some of the emotions that provoked criticism in the Cambuslang revival originated under the ministry of a "humanly ineffectual" minister, William McCullough. Dallimore describes the emotions: "They were of two kinds—the outcrying and trembling among the unconverted and the ecstatic joy among believers. . . . Indeed, such joy was more a part of this work than the sorrow over sin. It appears that many believers found themselves so moved by a sense of the Saviour's love to them and, in turn, by their new love in him, as to be lifted almost into a state of rapture."[9]

Sinners were moved by the Holy Spirit so "as to be lifted almost into a state of rapture." They were moved by what they described as a new sense of "the Saviour's love to them." It was not that they had no previous knowledge of the Savior's love, but that with hearts quickened by the Spirit they perceived it with a new and overwhelming clarity. Joy burst from their hearts and along with joy, praise of an almost ecstatic intensity.

In New Hampshire, as in Scotland, the same joy was born. Edwards writes: "Their joyful surprise has caused their hearts as it were to leap, so that they have been ready to break forth into laughter, tears often at the same time issuing like a flood, and intermingling a loud weeping."[10]

Ready to "break forth into laughter"? Joy is one thing, but laughter is something else. Yet I have heard people break into laughter when the Holy Spirit touches them, and they are astonishing to observe. The first time I encountered the phenomenon was in the notorious "Signs and Wonders" class at Fuller Seminary in 1984. Wimber had prayed that the Holy Spirit would equip a number of pastors and missionaries for the work God had called them to do. A South African pastor began to giggle and couldn't stop.

I might have supposed him to be reacting to something incongruous, either in the prayer or in the situation. It was the kind of giggle you associate with someone whose emotional "funny bone" has been touched. But there was a significant difference. People are embarrassed when they "get the giggles," but this man seemed oblivious to the rest of us. His face was open and he was smiling broadly. He seemed unaware that we did not share his secret. He continued to giggle, I am told, for several hours, waking during the night to do so. We were seeing his personal reaction to being "surprised by joy."

I have observed the same phenomenon several times since. When it is genuine it follows a similar pattern—irrepressibility, unself-consciousness. Often it continues intermittently for a long time. It seems to be associated with a beginning of release of tension in uptight people.

But there is also an imitation. "Holy laughter" in some circles carries prestige. To get the godly giggles or to produce it in others becomes a mark of spiritual achievement. Under those circumstances one detects a sense of strain. The laughter can be forced and distasteful.

But we must not shun the true because we fear the false. As I quoted Edwards earlier, "Though there are false affections in religion, and in some respects raised high: yet undoubtedly there are true, holy, and solid affections; and the higher these are raised the better. And when they are raised to an exceeding great height, they are not to be suspected merely because of their degree, but on the contrary to be esteemed."[11]

Trembling and Shaking

So far we have been looking at emotional manifestations, and emotional manifestations seem to be all that eighteenth-century writers ever saw. That is not to say that the same manifestations did not occur then that occur now, but that eighteenth-century writers seem to assume that what they observed was a reaction to consciously experienced emotion. Tears were from grief, ecstasy from joy, trembling from fear, with fainting or falling also from fear or shock. And in many cases this is how it seems to work. But not always.

Take the relationship between fear and trembling, for example. People in revivals do indeed tremble from fear, but others experience trembling in the absence of fear. I know a woman who trembles frequently (as with Parkinsonism) when she prays for other people. She is an emotionally stable woman whose testimony I respect. She describes the experience in terms of energy coursing through her. The phenomenon began in a meeting she attended where the Holy Spirit was powerfully present. While she cannot as it were produce the trembling or the "energy," when it comes she has the choice either of resisting it, or else of directing it (into prayer, for example). If she does the latter, she experiences a sensation of pulsating energy extending to her finger tips, along with a slight tremor in her hands. Her impression is of energy flowing through her. "You know those anatomical diagrams of the cardiovascular system? It feels as though the energy is flowing along those channels. . . ."

If the energy has something to do with the Holy Spirit (and I believe it has), it is important to note that her own control is limited to accepting or rejecting what God is doing. She does not take the initiative. Nor does she make any effort to enter into a trance state. Even her ability to accept or reject is by no means complete, being more a learning how to respond. She does not see her experience as the norm for other Christians and does not bother herself with trying to explain it.

For others (such as my wife and the people I described in an earlier chapter) the trembling (over which there is initially no control, though control often develops gradually over time) may continue intermittently for months. With the trembling there seems to be no fear, but more of quiet joy mingled with a strange peace.

Trembling varies in its intensity. At times in public meetings people are seized with violent shaking. Occasionally I have been astounded at the power and violence of the shaking. Such people do not shake, but are shaken, like rag dolls in the teeth of a terrier, their bodies moving backward and forward or from side to side, and their arms and sometimes even their legs flailing in the wake of their moving bodies. I doubt that any ballet dancer or gymnast could reproduce the movements, for the astounding thing is that while some people collapse and fall, the most violent maintain their equilibria.

More commonly a man's trunk may remain immobile, while the head may shake backward and forward (banging the wall behind in a regular rhythm if they should happen to be leaning against it). The arms, bent at the elbow, usually with palms facing the ground, flap violently up and down, from shoulders, elbows and wrist, the most violent movements being commonly at the wrist joint, while the hands flail so quickly as sometimes to dissolve into a blur. The movements are cyclical in intensity, rising repeatedly in slow waves to a crescendo, then subsiding again. Each cycle may last up to two or three minutes. Commonly, crescendos of activity coincide all over the gathering, though it is certain that affected persons are unaware of what other people are doing.

In frontier camp meetings this would be referred to as "the jerks."

Sometimes the subject of the jerks would be affected in some one member of the body, and sometimes in the whole system. When the head alone was affected, it would be jerked backward and forward, or from side to side, so quickly that the features of the face could not be distinguished. When the whole system was affected, I have seen the person stand in one place, and jerk backward and forward in quick succession, their hands nearly touching the floor behind and after. . . .

I have inquired of those thus affected. They could not account for it; but some have told me that those were among the happiest seasons of their lives. I have seen some wicked persons thus affected, and all the time cursing the jerks while they were thrown to the ground with a violence. Though so awful to behold I do not remember that any of the thousands I have seen ever sustained an injury in body. This was as strange as the accident itself.[12]

Though people affected by shaking are conscious and know where they are, they seem to be in a dazed and dreamlike state. Their sense of time is commonly impaired, in that they may not have a clear idea of how long their manifestation lasted. When waves of movement subside they will usually respond briefly to questions, though their ability to describe the experience through which they are passing is often limited to a physical description. ("My arms keep shaking. I can't stop them.") They may experience fear but usually do not. One man told me, "I just felt an enormous compassion . . . for people."

One variety of shaking that has been described to me, but that I have never seen personally, is called pogo-sticking. Sometimes the bodily shaking is on a vertical axis, the body leaving the ground in a series of bounces. Since the body remains more or less rigid, it looks like someone bouncing on a pogo stick.

The physical energy used must be considerable, especially when one considers that pogo-sticking is no respecter of persons. Yet no bodily harm seems to have occurred from pogo-sticking. Some years ago as the Holy Spirit's power fell during prayer in an Anglican church in the north of England, the rector fell forward on his face, and several staid members of the congregation (including the church wardens) began to pogo-stick.

Jonathan Edwards describes what could be pogo-sticking. "Since this time [a visit by Whitefield] there have often been great agitations of body, and an unavoidable leaping for joy. . . ."[13]

Falling

In almost every church I visited on a recent visit to Argentina people asked me, "¿Qué es eso de caerse?" (Roughly—"What's all this business of falling about?") They were referring to what was happening in the meetings of Carlos Annacondia. Newspaper and magazine reports were full of accounts of the many people who fell to the ground during his meetings. More dramatic still, some fell on their way to the meetings, while others were reported to fall from their seats in buses that were passing by the meetings.

At some point in the nineteenth century this particular phenomenon began to be called "being slain in the spirit." In eighteenth-century accounts it is "being overcome" or "fainting." In the Bible it is, "fell at his feet as though dead" (Rev 1:17), "drew back and fell to the ground" (Jn 18:6) and "fell on my face" (Dan 10:9 RSV). It is not one phenomenon but many. It may occur gently or violently, be associated with great distress or profound calm.

In 1982, in Birmingham, England, during his second visit to Britain, John Wimber was at a prayer meeting in a Baptist church.

About thirty people were present including a small ministry team from the United States. Wimber, who frequently prays with his eyes open, began to pray and had got as far as word, "Lord—" when he saw (in what seemed to be like slow motion) a Black man lifted into the air. The man looked as though he were being lifted and laid briefly on an invisible stretcher, before sailing back to crash heavily into several chairs as he screamed, "Hallelujah!" Wimber was afraid that the violence of the fall would have killed him, but the man was unhurt.

Falls are commonly much less violent and may be backward (common) or forward (less common and in my observation more frequent in pastors and ministers). Falls may be associated with further violent movements, with head-banging, tremors, movements suggestive of epilepsy, but commonly with a total absence of movement. Subjects may have no experience beyond a pleasant sense of calm, may experience visions, or may feel that they are being crushed. One man told me he felt as though a massive weight was crushing the life out of him, making it impossible for him to breathe and giving him the feeling that he was "being squeezed out like a tube of toothpaste."

Many people may be affected simultaneously. When this is so, the precise timing suggests supernatural choreography rather than mass hysteria. Crowd effect may sometimes be postulated when, for example, the phenomenon has become known in a country or locality. But there have been many times when no one anticipated what would happen and when people had no opportunity to see or be influenced by what others were doing. Everyone fell together.

John Strazosich is a Fuller graduate with a charismatic background. He had previously experienced the "baptism of the Spirit" and had spoken in tongues. In January 1985, he attended the Vineyard Christian Fellowship in Los Osos, and during the ministry time asked for "more power." Slowly, beginning with one arm, a shaking took possession of his whole body. Soon he was shaking violently and continued to shake for two hours.

He had the feeling that at any time he could have stopped what was happening, though he was sure that he was not producing the shaking himself. However, believing God was ministering to him, he prayed that God would enable him to minister in different ways. With each request for more the shaking increased in violence. Finally, he could stand no more, and asked God to stop. His muscles ached for three days afterward.

"After that, every time I prayed for someone they would fall down. It went on for some months. When God spoke to me it was very clear. It's not that clear anymore, not as clear as it was—but it was real clear then."

Some days later at a Christian camp he began to "bounce up and down" from a standing position. "God told him" to start praying for some of the young men around him. It was difficult to speak, and he had difficulty in explaining his intentions, it not being easy to speak coherently when bouncing. He prayed for three young men, barely touching them before they fell to the ground. A fourth boy shook, "but was not receiving anything." He was "resistant" because of his desire to heed the lyrics of certain rock songs. A fifth fellow was affected by laughter. Eventually John himself was no longer able to remain standing, and fell to the ground.

The unusual effects of his praying led to a very embarrassing situation. One Sunday after church John and two friends went to the Marriott Hotel in Anaheim to have supper at the La Plaza restaurant there. They were told they would have a twenty-minute wait. In the lobby John proceeded to tell his friends what had been happening in his life. He noticed a man in the lobby and thought he sensed God telling him to pray for the man, but he was uncertain. Eventually the man approached him, having overheard the conversation. He was a Canadian. "That was interesting to listen to." It turned out that the man was attending a conference led by pentecostal preacher and healer Maurice Cerillo. John asked him whether he wanted John to pray for him.

The man agreed, and John, fearful of a scene in the lobby, suggested they go outside. Outside on the sidewalk by some bushes he prayed, and the man fell backward into the bushes, his legs protruding on to the sidewalk. John was uncertain what he should do next? In church at the Vineyard there would be an appropriate way of handling the situation. But not here.

So he did what he had done before. He bent down and began to "bless whatever God was doing." As he did so he heard footsteps approaching and turned to see two security agents bearing down on him, "Stop! Security."

John stood and took a couple of paces toward the men, realizing they thought that he had been mugging the man on the ground. "I wasn't mugging the guy! I was praying for him—and God did that." Slowly and semistuporous, the man on the ground had begun to get up. "Tell them I was praying for you!"

The man complied, "Yes—he was just praying . . ."

"Well, we don't allow that around here!"

John protested. "But I can't stop God . . ."

"What are you doing here anyway?"

"I'm waiting to eat in the restaurant."

The security agent turned to the Canadian. "And what are you doing?"

"I'm a guest at the hotel."

The agents stared at each other and shook their heads. After a further admonition to the two men, they turned and left them.

Most people who fall are at least partially aware of their surroundings and have a sense of the passage of time. But their sense of time (like Rip Van Winkle's) is impaired. I have received reports such as, "I thought I had been 'out' about fifteen minutes—but it was nearer two hours," or, "It felt like just a few minutes, but when I came to I was still real groggy, and I'd been on the floor for four hours. Nearly everyone had gone home. I was real surprised."

Visions
Not infrequently people who fall report visions. Skepticism about

the validity of these is understandable, and caution should be exercised in attaching significance to every reported vision. But some are undoubtedly from God.

At a prayer meeting in New York at the beginning of the decade, participants were interceding for the city when a young man received a vision, the details of which he later revealed. He saw hands offering him a bowl or cup to drink. Into the bowl had been poured the vileness of the sins of New York. The young man cried out, "No, no!" turning his head away and attempting to push the cup from him.

Instantly he was struck to the ground. A heaviness fell on all the approximately seventy-five participants, who without exception also fell to the ground. John Wimber, who was present, remembers a sense of heaviness that he was unable to support, that made him slump to the ground, where he remained sobbing, along with many others, as he prayed for the city.

The young man has for several years now been walking the streets of New York ministering powerfully to the homeless and to alcoholics, drug addicts, prostitutes and others. The genuineness of the vision is attested in this case by its results. A young man was thrust into an effective gospel ministry of a kind that few of us would choose. The ministry has brought no personal glory or prestige to him. The vision he received also had a profound moral significance. It had to do with a horror of the vile sins of a city, and the call of the evangelist or prophet to know that horror in experience.

It was the moral and ethical quality as well as the emphasis on a divine solution to the moral dilemma that distinguished John's visions in Revelation from the mass of spurious visions in the apocalyptic literature of his day. The imagery was very similar, much of it being drawn from Daniel's prophetic writings. But unlike the book of Revelation, the rest of the literature is merely predictive. There is a notable absence of any concern about sin and righteousness or a need for redemption. This precise note in the young man's vision also suggests the vision's authenticity.

Demonic Manifestations

As discussed earlier, the powers of darkness may imitate many divine supernatural acts. As we shall see again later, this became evident long ago when Moses found himself face to face with the magicians of Egypt (Ex 7:8-13, 20-22; 8:5-7). Therefore the form the manifestation takes is not a reliable guide to what is taking place.

Shaking has been seen when the Holy Spirit comes on people. It is also a recognized sign of a demonic trance. "Doc Anderson" collaborates with certain oil-well drillers. His hands shake, stigmata appear and where the blood drips, oil is found. I have seen his performances on TV, and of course it could be faked (except that there is the little matter of productive oil wells dug where experts had declared there could be no oil).

I can think of many other instances that could cause confusion. For instance, consider the rapid side-to-side movement of the head that makes the face a blur. I have only seen this once. It was in a Singapore church. At the name of Jesus a demonized man was flung several feet, landing on his hands and knees before what I believe was a communion table. His nose must have been no more than a millimeter from a sharp corner of the table, and his head was thrashing with frightening violence from side to side, with a range of movement that seemed to exceed what is normal and at a speed that made his features a blur.

At the time I assumed that those particular movements must be characteristic of demonization; that is, that wherever they might appear they would be a sure sign a demon was around. I am more cautious now. Having seen some of the strange ways in which people react to the power of the Holy Spirit, the man's movements could have been a demonic imitation of something real. Chapter six examines this problem in more detail.

Demons do, however, have certain characteristic ways of manifesting themselves. The most obvious are verbal expressions of defiance and hostility (commonly in a changed voice). I remember sitting in the pastor's office of a Baptist church counseling a woman, when from the other side of the church I heard a man's voice roaring in rage. When I went out to see what was happening I saw my wife and a colleague ministering to a lady who at that point was huddled in a pew. The defiance had come from a demon they had just cast out of the woman.

Not infrequently when I pray for someone in a meeting, the person will immediately go into a trancelike state. Eyes may roll back, the person may fall, may begin to make epileptiform movements—may even foam and dribble mucus from his or her mouth. The signs are not necessarily a proof of a demon (the person may be having a grand mal seizure). Usually at that point I demand in the name of Jesus that any demon who might be present give me its name. Once the demon does so, I know where I am and can act accordingly.

On one occasion when I addressed a demon I suspected was present in a woman, the woman (she herself was shocked by what happened) suddenly writhed toward me feet first, reared up and hissed in my face. I would say that the manifestation, symbolically serpentine, was characteristically demonic. But there is room for more careful research in this area.

Sometimes in Wimber's meetings there may be a scream or a commotion either during the message or else when people are praying for some present. Often this is an indication of demonic activity. An experienced team usually tries to conduct the victim to a quiet, secluded area where he or she may be appropriately helped.

Drunk with the Spirit

In meetings where the Holy Spirit's power is strongly manifest, some people may seem a little drunk. However, I have never seen them noisy or obstreperous in this state. They may describe a "heaviness" that is on them. Their speech may be slightly slurred, their movements uncoordinated. They may need support to walk. They show little concern about what anyone will think of their condition and are usually a little dazed. In the previous chapter I suggested that the drowsiness of the apostles on the Mount of Transfiguration may have had such an explanation. The condition may endure several hours.

Is it possible that Paul's words in Ephesians 5:18 refer to such a state? Obviously being filled with the Spirit is preferable to being drunk, however one understands the verse. But it is possible that two kinds of "drunkenness" are being compared.

If so I would like to have seen what happened at Pentecost. The apostles were certainly speaking in recognizable languages, and evidently without any Galilean accent. But did some of them seem a little drunk? People do not usually accuse others of being drunk unless something about the performance suggests it. If you see an uneducated man whose eye is clear and whose movements are well controlled talking in a recognizable language, drunkenness is not the first explanation that comes into your head. It is possible that what happened to some of them was what I have observed in many other people on whom the Spirit rests.

The Central Question

A reading of the history of revivals will bring to light many other forms of manifestation. Anyone interested in traveling widely and recording what is currently taking place will undoubtedly add much to what I have recorded above. How worthwhile such research would be is debatable. The central question has to do with whether God is active or not, and on whether revival could be beginning. And on this I have made my opinion clear.

If I am right, what are the implications for each one of us personally? My aim is not to promote manifestations so much as to encourage us all to be open to what God is doing and to what I believe he wants to do in sending revival. I don't want you to close your mind to what God may be doing or to go chasing after unusual experiences under a misapprehension that you need to be "zapped" to be revived. Unusual experiences are by definition not part of normal discipleship. If God should have an unusual experience in store for you, and if that should help your relationship with God, well and good. But the experience itself is neither here nor there, except as being an evidence that God is moving in revival. It is your relationship with God that matters.

Revivals make people holy. Your goal and mine must be to pursue God himself and to let him make us holy. It must be to inquire whether further steps of obedience are called for in some area of our lives where we may have been closed to him. It must also be to collaborate with his purposes by praying according to his will. And to pray like that means that we must know what God wants to do in our time.

Therefore, let me pursue my inquiry about manifestations. There are other questions that must be considered. Why do some people react one way, others in different ways and many of us not at all? Do particular movements tell us anything about the personalities, the sins, the specific problems in those people to whom they happen? I shall try to answer such questions in the next chapter.

8
Why Do Revival Experiences Differ So Much?

T HE WIND BLOWS WHEREVER IT PLEASES. *You hear its sound, but you cannot tell where it comes from or where it is going." JESUS*

Three questions faced me as I began to examine behavioral manifestations in revival. The first was a general question about all the manifestations. *Were they from God or should they only be viewed in psychological or sociological terms?* This was the topic of earlier chapters.

The second and more specific question had to do with the individual form the Spirit-induced manifestations took. *If such manifestations are indeed the work of the Spirit, how do we account for the different forms they may take?* I began with the naive assumption that they would lie open to human analysis. Trembling would mean one thing, falling flat on one's back one thing and falling prone another, weeping something more obvious yet—and so on. But the more I have interviewed affected people and pondered over their stories, the more mysterious the matter has become. To force my observations into a coherent theory is at present impossible. I suspect that even rigorous research would not clarify the mystery.

I am reminded of an early sermon by D. Martyn Lloyd-Jones: "As with the wind, the evidence of which we see in the results— the rustle of leaves and the sway of branches—so the way in which the Holy Spirit moves men. Though certain and sure, it is beyond analysis."[1]

The third question is one that onlookers often ask. *Why are some people affected and not others?*

Individual Differences

If there is a guiding principle in understanding what happens when God touches someone, it seems to be that God treats people as individuals, each having a unique history, unique problems and a unique calling from his or her Creator. And what on the surface might appear to be a mass reaction turns out on examination to cover the unique and mysterious dealings of a Creator with his creatures. Therefore only by understanding a given individual could I hope to perceive anything at all of the mysterious operations of the Spirit.

I must make one thing quite clear, however. Manifestations take place during revivals. Those Christians whose spiritual progress has been quiet and steady may never, even where the power of the Holy Spirit is present, be subject to any manifestation. The fact that God in inscrutable wisdom deals in this way with some people does not mean that if you have not trembled or been thrown on the floor, then you are inadequate as a Christian. To be sure, all of us need to be empowered and anointed by the Spirit, but that empowering does not need to be dramatic, as I shall discuss more fully in the final chapter.

Let me give an extract from John Mumford's diary to illustrate the idiosyncratic nature of manifestations. John is an English clergyman currently serving as an assistant pastor in the Vineyard Fellowship in Anaheim. He has permitted me to quote from his diary, where he describes vividly his experience during John Wimber's meetings in Sheffield in 1985.

On the last night of the Sheffield conference before the final session, I was in the process of having supper with Rick and Lulu Williams in the hotel when, again unexpectedly, John and Carol joined us. We were all talking about this and that, and after John McLure had (again) joined us, John W began to talk a little about the future. It was strange, because I felt the pain—absent for two or three days—come back along with (all I can call) a stirring, an excitement, a deep feeling that this is "it," this is what I'm called to do, what God put me here to do. It sounds grandiose, but it wasn't.

During the final meeting . . . John W began to talk about the church for about three quarters of an hour. As he spoke, I felt increasingly that same pain, but also as if someone had their hand on the middle of my chest and were pressing down hard— the pressure/pain was quite distinct and—in my experience— unique. There was a coffee break at about 9:00 pm, but I simply had no energy or inclination to get up—I just sat there. At one point Becky Cook came across to ask me to do something or other, but I made excuses and told her of my pain. When I explained further she just smiled and said simply: "You need to stay there."

Immediately after the break we all stood, and John invited the Holy Spirit to come—and sure enough he did! What followed was the most extraordinary thing I think I have ever experienced in my whole life.

The Spirit came on me, and my head fell forward a bit. Then

as the intensity grew, my hands became heavy and cramped and "frozen" and "paralyzed" like two claws, and then that spread to the rest of my torso. The "tautness" all over me reminded me of the old Westerns where the bad guy gets bitten by a rattlesnake, his body then "tenses" and contorts before he finally keels over.

(Becky Cook and Rick and Lulu Williams prayed for me all this time.) As time went on my brain began to throb inside my head, then my hands went limp, folded across my groin as I bent over, until finally I fell on to my knees and ultimately, prostrate lying headlong on the carpet.

My whole body kept on twitching and heaving—I can only describe it as "retching" air, having vomited everything out of one's stomach—and gasping. It was as if the air and very breath was being expelled from me—like lifesavers do to expel water from the lungs of someone who's nearly drowned. There was groaning, gasping, crying out too, and tingling in feet and hands.

At one point I was aware of John and Carol praying over me, and Becky again. I had a word about having a "bit" in my mouth, as in a bridled horse.

Before I actually keeled over, I suddenly felt terrified that I'd "missed it" and I remember begging Becky not to stop, and then a bit later heard myself praying—as I sank to my knees—aloud: "Lord, don't let me get away this time; nail me, nail me; keep me on a short rein, a short leash; you can't trust me; I'm not to be trusted." There was one phrase going through my mind over and over again, "Kill me, Kill me . . ."

I can only describe the whole thing as a process of dying. I felt afterward like Sir Walter Raleigh's cloak after Queen Elizabeth had walked over it; or I felt like I'd been rolled over by a steam roller! God had sat on me.

The whole thing must have lasted one and a half hours and by the end I felt blitzed. I lay on my back for what seemed a long time, unable to move, with my arms outstretched on the floor in a cruciform shape—if it's not blasphemy, the significance was not lost upon me.

Eventually, they sat me up at 11:00 pm and I staggered out, feeling totally dazed, propped up on either side by Carol and Colin Wooldrich, back to the hotel.

That night in bed and again next morning, I felt the Spirit on me—the energy, the trembling, feeling as if my body was quaking and shaking inside, tho' it wasn't outwardly. All I can say by way of explanation at this point is that it was a visitation by the Holy Spirit—by passing the mind maybe for no other purpose than to establish and deepen my relationship with the Lord.

What was fascinating to discover later was that, as I lay on the floor between 9-11 pm, Eleanor was in bed in Scotland, and as she cried out to the Lord, he gave her Isaiah 55:1-3—"Why spend money on what is not bread, and your labour on what does not satisfy?"

Before we ask what God was doing with John Mumford, let us ask a prior question. Was God doing anything at all? Might there not be a more mundane explanation of John's experience? Was he perhaps being hysterical? Could some of the symptoms have arisen from hyperventilation? And if the manifestation came from God, what was God doing?

John Mumford is a cheerful, energetic Englishman, happily married and (at the time of the diary entry) the father of one child. He enjoyed his calling as an Anglican minister, though at the time of the diary entry was wondering whether God might be leading him into a different ministry. He knew that not all his friends might understand the move. To what extent does an understanding of the reaction lie in the crisis (if such it was) that he was facing?

Let us begin with the question of an hysterical attack. John told me that his mood during what appeared to be a horrendous ordeal was almost detached, as though he were observing the distress of someone else, even though he was aware that it was all happening to him. His remark might at first suggest hysteria. In hysterical states there is a sign referred to as *belle indiference*. Hysterical patients suffering, say, from total paralysis, will describe their inability to move, but display strange indifference to such a shocking disability while discussing it.

But hysterical patients (whose personalities differ radically from John Mumford's) never tell you that they feel a sense of detachment. The detachment is something the observer notices and is something the patient is unaware of. John's remark displays insight into his emotional state at the time, whereas hysterical patients are singularly lacking in insight about why they behave the way they do.

A second interesting point concerns his volition—his own will about what was happening. He told me that he felt that at any time he could have broken the state in which he found himself (again, not the sort of observation a hysterical person would make). Whether his impression is correct will never be known. Many people on whom the Spirit falls have absolutely no choice in the matter. They are knocked flat. Others, like Saul of Tarsus, find their wills turned right about-face in a moment. Nevertheless John Mumford's impression is interesting.

Any interaction of divine power and human weakness raises the age-old and never-solved problem of divine sovereignty in relation to human responsibility. Could John have effectively resisted what God was doing? What credit might he claim for his own part in what took place? I believe John could have resisted what God was doing. But I have observed, and Scripture affirms, that some people are totally impotent. Certainly King Saul was impotent when he lay on the ground naked before Samuel and David.

We have already seen that equally powerful manifestations may produce profound spiritual changes in some people, and none at all—or at least none that are discernible—in others. And this suggests to me that the Spirit's action calls at some level for a human response, conscious or unconscious, and that the response is essential to the result. It seems that the spiritual aftereffects of such a manifestation are dependant on the subject's willingness to let God have his way.

Perhaps if John had broken off what was happening in the early stages, the weakness and exhaustion that came later might not have supervened since some of it undoubtedly resulted from the muscular exertion involved. But of one thing John Mumford was certain. While he might have been able to resist the physical manifestation, he was not producing the symptoms himself. He was not their source.

Some of his symptoms may have been related to his breathing. He writes, "My hands became heavy and cramped and 'frozen' and 'paralysed' like two claws, and then that spread to the rest of my torso. The 'tautness' all over me reminded me of the old Westerns where the bad guy gets bitten by a rattlesnake, his body then 'tenses' and contorts before he finally keels over." This description fits some of the symptoms that occur when one is breathing too quickly, thereby reducing blood carbon-dioxide levels. Indeed at one point he speaks of tingling in his hands and feet. If we were trying to debunk the story we could say that John Mumford was merely having a hyperventilation attack. He was anxious. He was facing a radical life change—a new direction in his ministry. What could be more understandable under such circumstances?

But the explanation would be too facile. Anxiety may well be a part of the picture, but if so the anxiety has to do with something deeper. He had gone through radical changes before—his marriage, his call to the ministry for example, and had experienced nothing of the sort then. The clue lies in his desperate plea to God, " 'Lord, don't let me get away this time; nail me, nail me; keep me on a short rein, a short leash; you can't trust me; I'm not to be trusted.' There was one phrase going through my mind over and over again, 'Kill me, kill me. . . .' "

This seems to be a key. It only incidentally had to do with a possible change in his circumstances. It had much more to do with his relationship with God.

John had a problem common to many of us. He was aware of conflicting desires within himself—the desire to be completely the Lord's and the desire to hang on to some personal rights. His relationship with God was threatened by what he perceived as his own weakness and inconstancy. He feared that he might run away from a depth of commitment God required of him. An easier path might prove too strong a temptation. He was desperately anxious that this should not happen. Hence his plea to Becky to continue in prayer and his own prayer to be "nailed," to be "killed" so that it would be impossible for him to betray his commitment to the will of God.

The "word" of which he speaks is a "word of knowledge," a term to describe a revelation from the Holy Spirit about one's own or someone else's personal need.[2] It concerned the bit in the mouths of horses. Whether he immediately understood the significance of the word is not clear. But somewhere deep down he was aware of a need for greater control over himself, the same control an experienced rider has over a horse.

John Mumford's physical reactions represented the result of a unique operation of the Holy Spirit. We may never know all that the Spirit was doing. Among other things he was being equipped and empowered for future service. But the pattern of his commissioning was idiosyncratic, having to do with his personal problems and needs.

The pattern that emerged was symbolic. The life of self-will he might have lived was being crushed out of him. He was indeed being "nailed." Like the slave who did not want to be set free he had declared, "I love my master . . . and do not want to go free." God had pierced his ear through with an awl and made him a servant for life (Ex 21:5-6). His cruciform posture on the ground was not blasphemy but a sign to him, and to anyone else who cared to see, that he was crucified with Christ so that he might live to serve without fear.

This leads us to my third question, one I began to answer earlier.

Why do some of us experience no dramatic manifestations? Why are such manifestations peculiar only to certain people in times of revival? Isn't what John craved what so many of us crave? Why then should God do something to John Mumford and not to the rest of us?

Again I have only a partial answer. First, let me say that if a spiritual work was done in John (and his life certainly manifests that it has), it is only one stage in an ongoing process that we hope will continue for the rest of his life. John has not "arrived." Nor is it necessary to lie on the floor feeling air being forced out of one in order for God to deal with one's ambivalence. God has dealt with many people in a less dramatic manner. Earlier I pointed out that the Holy Spirit's work in times of revival is accelerated. What at other times may be done silently, progressively and less dramatically may be done instantaneously and with a demonstration of power in times of revival.

There is another factor operating here. I call it the ripening factor. In all our lives there seems to be a time when God deals with specific issues. We may struggle for years with a problem, aware that a particular sin need not have dominion over us, yet repeatedly we may fail to throw off the sin. And then after years, the sin, like an evil, overripe fruit, drops to the ground often with a flash of inner-illumination. Suddenly we are free. What all along was true theologically becomes true in our experience.

And whether in times of revival or in more normal times, the Spirit's operations remain unique. He decides to change one person one way and make the same change in a different person a different way. He also knows when one person is ready for change while another may need more time. It is we who demand stereotypes, wanting him to be predictable in the way he deals with us all.

Sometimes the form of the manifestation has nothing to do with the person affected. When the Holy Spirit fell on King Saul he prophesied. Presumably that was one way observers could tell what was happening, since ecstatic prophecy seems to have been a widely recognized phenomenon. Similarly when the Holy Spirit fell on the household of Cornelius it was important that Peter realize what was happening. For that reason the manifestation on that occasion was one of speaking in tongues, the significance of which Peter could not fail to understand.

The Shaping of the Reaction
I have said before that the form of a manifestation itself may not tell us much about what is taking place spiritually inside someone. Yet individual factors do have some influence. For example: (1) personality type; (2) specific unresolved sins; (3) specific problems from the past; (4) the presence of evil spirits; and (5) God's order of events. Let us consider each of these in turn.

1. *The Effect of Personality.* Our personalities tend to determine the form in which we react to anything. The same verse of Scripture will be received by one person with enthusiasm, by another with anxiety, by yet another with suspicion. Some people are more open, others more closed, some more responsive, others more controlled. Their reactions are determined not only by their views of Scripture, but also by their natures. Their friends could have predicted their responses beforehand.

It should not surprise us, therefore, to find that people's responses to close contact with the Holy Spirit's power may vary, and that differences may in part reflect differences in personality.

A skeptical young German theological student began to manifest the power of the Holy Spirit as Wimber prayed for him during a February 1984 lecture at Fuller Seminary. "I feel nothing," he replied in response to a question from Wimber. To Wimber it was obvious that bodily reactions were occurring in the man, yet he insisted in a somewhat contradictory manner. "I can't sit down. I can't move. I don't feel anything and I can't move." Initially the rigidity of his personality had made him insensitive to what was happening to him.

The case is extreme but it illustrates the extent to which our personalities and habits of mind may affect our response to whatever the Holy Spirit may be doing, and even to the form a reaction may take.

2. *The Effect of Specific Sins.* Certain writhing bodily movements seem to reflect conflict over a particular sin or bondage, often a sexual sin. While it is unwise to jump to conclusions on observing bodily writhing, a number of subjects who experienced such movements went on to confess and deal with such sins as they were being prayed for.

It would be unwise, however, to jump to premature conclusions about bodily movements. We need to be cautious about becoming expert interpreters of symptoms.

3. *The Effect of Problems in the Past.* On one occasion my wife and I prayed for the healing of a woman who had a long-standing bowel condition that caused passage of blood and mucus. As we were praying, her limbs began to jerk convulsively. She began to weep and suddenly cry out, "It's all right, Henry. I forgive you! It doesn't matter any more!"

We knew nothing of the conflict to which she referred, and she told us little afterward, mentioning only that it had to do with a brother who had sinned against her. Not only was she healed immediately of her illness, but two different members of her church commented spontaneously on the subsequent change in her personality. She displayed a new and unaccustomed gentleness and warmth.

4. *The Effect of Occult Influences.* In the previous chapter I discussed demonization briefly. The condition will sometimes (but not always) determine the form of the manifestation. Occult influences can operate in a variety of ways.

A former member of the Children of God would begin to bite her hands whenever people prayed for her. She bit her hands "to stop myself from saying anything," but was at a loss to know why she would need to do so. It eventually came to light that during her stay in West Africa a witch doctor there had been paid by a jealous woman to place a curse on her. Once prayer was made for the curse to be broken, she was simultaneously healed from a major and "incurable" illness and released from the urge to bite her hands during prayer.

5. *God's Unique Plan for the Individual.* Another young woman who attended a Vineyard conference in Georgia headed by Blaine Cooke wanted healing for a bone disease. The healing did not take place. However, as prayer was made for those in need (not specifically for healing) she fell to the ground overwhelmed. God dealt with her attitude toward him and others. She subsequently displayed an unaccustomed willingness to be responsible for her own work and to help others.

God had done a powerful work in her, but his priorities were not hers. His first priority for her was a change of heart.

The Limits of Science

It became evident to me soon after I began to watch the powerful effects of the Holy Spirit on people's bodies, that the simple notions with which I began would have to be discarded. If scientific investigation were to throw any light on the strange variations in them, and on why they took one form in one individual and another in someone else, a fairly time-consuming and complex study would be necessary. The study would need the work of a team of experienced investigators in different centers using standardized descriptions of manifestations and thorough analysis of the personalities and life histories of persons in whom they occurred. Ideally it would be a prospective study, one in which all the people concerned would be followed over a considerable period of time.

Such a study would be very costly in time, energy and money. Would the findings be worth the effort? I am inclined to doubt it, though certainly there are many Christian psychologists and psychiatrists who spend time and money studying less worthwhile questions. My own purpose in making this simple inquiry is to satisfy myself whether many things that are happening currently represent a work of God of the kind that occurs during times of revival.

In any case I always have felt that, J. B. Rhine notwithstanding,[3] any scientific investigation of supernatural events is fraught with insuperable difficulties. I pointed some of them out in January 1975, at a symposium on demonism held on the campus of the University of Notre Dame under the sponsorship of the Christian Medical Society.

Good research begins when you delineate what you want to find out when you define precisely what it is you want to know. And if what we want to know concerns the work of the Holy Spirit, we will have to know to what extent the Holy Spirit determines what happens. How much of Johnny's weeping comes from his childhood experiences, and how much from the work of the Holy Spirit? To measure the Holy Spirit would not seem to me to be an appropriate activity for Christians, even if it could be done. And I for one would never try.

In the book *Demon Possession*, I expressed the problem in the case of demonism as follows:

Diagnosis presents us with a thorny problem. . . . In the absence of scriptural diagnostic principles we are forced to fall back either on the direct illuminations of the Holy Spirit to guide us in a given case, or else devise rules based on experimental evidence.

My own conviction is that science is helpless in the face of the diagnostic problem. I can conceive of no demonic state which cannot be "explained" by a non-demonic hypothesis. . . . [So instead of calling a given condition demonic] we could ask the question: What is the most effective method of changing blasphemous outbursts of rage?

We would have to assign blasphemers randomly to different treatment methods—exorcism, counseling, psychotherapy (and ideally to a control group also), a procedure which raises both technical and moral difficulties.

If we did not assign subjects randomly to different groups, the subjects would choose the method they believed in most. In that case we could not possibly rule out placebo effects. There is no way in which a single-blind, let alone a double-blind, study could be carried out. All the blasphemers would know what method was being used. And their faith in a given method would produce a placebo factor.[4]

Why the Repeats?

Some folk fall down (or tremble, shake, weep and so on) time after time. Why? Why do some people have one experience, when others have one after another? Perhaps John Mumford will be thrown on the floor again someday. But he shows no sign of it at present. I have watched him carefully over a period of a year in circumstances where he might be expected to perform if he were a "repeater." But no obvious manifestations hit John.

Yet some people continue to display manifestations over a period of months and a few give the impression of shaking or falling whenever there is an appropriate opportunity. Even though they are few, the fact that they repeat the performance regularly, usually on public occasions "biases the sample" of manifestations occurring at a particular time.

How should we view this? Ought responsible leaders to discourage more than one manifestation per person? Are we getting at the problem that caused so much controversy early in the eighteenth century? By what principles can we make decisions of this sort? Already I have stated that a minority of people who tremble, weep or fall may do so to attract attention, or to reassure themselves that the Lord still loves them.

Yet as I questioned repeaters I found the picture is more complex than I suspected. Most of the subjects I talked to were not histrionic. Some suffered from low self-esteem but were aware of it and had enough insight to evaluate their ongoing manifestations. I was sure that many I talked to were not reacting out of a psychological need to reassure themselves. In some subjects[5] there was a growing perception of the relationship between their inner attitudes and thoughts and the onset of a given manifestation. In others a series of visions producing insights about their relationship with God was bringing progressive change in their worship and their Christian walk.

Slowly I began to suspect that a powerful anointing of the Holy Spirit tends to produce among other things a new learned pattern of behavior with its own triggering mechanism. Our brains are incredible things. Endlessly they facilitate new interconnections among nerves as we learn new patterns of behavior. It is a process analogous to programming a computer. As we learn to drive, for instance, new "subroutines" governing semiautomatic behavior are established. As a result we will eventually be able to drive home, unconscious of scores of decisions we are making automatically as the "programmed subroutines" govern the movements of our hands, feet and eyes.

I do not know that this happens when someone is powerfully anointed by the Holy Spirit. But the evidence suggests it. Certainly some changes are made in us so that we can switch on or switch off behaviors the Holy Spirit inspires. What initially may have been impossible to control, progressively becomes easier to control. Paul assures us, for instance, that speaking in a tongue and uttering prophecies (the exercise of Spirit-imparted gifts) are under the voluntary control of individual Christians. The Spirit may inspire, but the Christian chooses when to utter. "If anyone speaks in a tongue, two—or at the most three—should speak, one at a time . . ." (1 Cor 14:27). "The spirits of prophets are subject to the control of prophets" (1 Cor 14:32).

Repeated manifestations are also under the voluntary control of the individual or become so within a relatively short time. This does not necessarily mean that they can "turn it on" whenever they choose, but that when the Holy Spirit is powerfully present they can choose to suppress or to allow the manifestation to take place.

It is as though the Holy Spirit's presence is the trigger which releases what I have called the subroutine, but that the triggering alone is not enough. The subject must choose to go along with what is happening.

In addition there is a tendency for phenomena to decrease progressively in power with the passage of time and to eventually disappear altogether in most people. With the disappearance a degree of elation and excitement that characterized the initial manifestations subsides also. And the process of the rise and progressive waning of the manifestation calls for no particular intervention on the part of church leaders.

There are people, however, who give way to the manifestations inappropriately and for the wrong reasons. Godfrey the Giggler (not his real name) is one. Godfrey is a forty-nine-year-old male who was converted four years ago, shortly after his third marriage. He works at an advertising agency in a large Texas city.

Godfrey is a short, talkative extrovert and is enthusiastic about everything he does. He was the only son of abusive, alcoholic parents, and he abused alcohol himself until his conversion. He feels that his childhood has left him with a number of identity problems but states, "I don't have any problem with self-esteem. I have got over that. I really like myself." However, his endless superficial chatter, name-dropping and boasting, mingled with anxious questioning about what I think of his opinions, give me the impression that he protests too much about liking himself and is actually very insecure.

In a May 1985 Wimber conference, he received a powerful anointing of the Holy Spirit which took the form of "holy laughter." At the time he experienced a great deal of relief from a neurotic sense of guilt and entered into a much deeper appreciation of the death of Christ and of the love of the Father. He continued on that occasion to laugh intermittently for almost thirty-six hours. It was evident that there was nothing put on about his laughter.

He subsequently attended every Vineyard conference he could, and frequently reported to me, "I got the holy laughter again. It was terrific. I got it first, then everybody else got it. We were all laughing like crazy." His letters bothered me, for it grew steadily clearer that "getting the laughter" and especially being the first person to "get" it had become a means by which Godfrey reassured himself about his personal worth. The Holy Spirit had elected him, as it were, to start the ball rolling. And this made it obvious to him that he was really important.

What was going on? Where did the Holy Spirit really come in? As I reflected on the problem in the half-awake, half-a-dream hour before dawn, I began to see that Godfrey's godly-giggling subroutine was probably being triggered whenever he was in contact with the Spirit's power and that he was only too happy to give expression to it because of his deep need for reassurance. It was then that I mentally dubbed him, Godfrey the Godly Giggler.

Soon after, I was present at a conference where laughter occurred. Most of the twelve hundred present were attending their first conference. Following an evening session there had been a palpable sense both of massive relief from absolved guilt and of exultation at the glory of Christ's triumphs. We were asked to stand and wait in the Lord together in silence.

A moment or two passed and someone began to laugh. The laughter spread in one sector of the auditorium. It did not seem altogether congruent with the prevailing mood, but I was not greatly disturbed. Wisely the worship leader began to lead in worship in song, and soon the whole congregation began to express vociferously their sense of glorying and exulting in the Christ's supremacy. The victory of Christ was our victory.

Later someone told me, "Godfrey started it again."

"It was? Oh, dear! I'm going to have to speak to him."

On that occasion nothing very serious happened. But can human beings react harmfully to the Holy Spirit? harmfully to themselves? to others? Can we abuse the power of the Holy Spirit?

Let us take up the theme in the next chapter.

9
How Safe Is Spiritual Power?

DO *NOT REJOICE THAT THE SPIRITS SUB-*
mit to you, but rejoice that your names are written in heaven." JESUS

The manifestations I have been talking about are manifestations of power. All power has dangers. The greater the power, the greater the danger. Pylons marching in single file carry their high-voltage electrical wires well above the ground. With them they bear signs with the word *DANGER* in red letters. Contact with the wires kills people.

The same atomic power that lights a city and fuels its industries can annihilate a city when it gets out of control. Chernobyl was a repeatable nightmare. The power under the hood of an ordinary automobile can kill and maim. Power always can be wrongly used. Spiritual power is no exception to the rule. God "took the risk" (though that is not the best way to express the matter, for he knew exactly what he was doing and what would follow) of giving plenty of it to Satan and the hosts of angels who rebelled. They absconded with the power he had bestowed on them and catastrophe followed. A cosmic war began that still continues. God even bestows power on fallible, immature human beings when he makes them his partners in the gospel. He has yet to invent a dangerproof power.

People who have never experienced the raw impact of spiritual power find it hard to understand that it could be dangerous. An experience of the impact of spiritual power can be compared with the experience of sexuality. People are never quite the same following their first sexual experience. A change has taken place in the way they see and will henceforth experience themselves, their world and other people. Nor is the change necessarily for the better. In fact it has equal potential for good and evil. All we can say is that a change has occurred. So it is with the experience of divine power.

Both have to do with experience. A virgin is a little like a blind person. Some virgins idealize sex. Others fear it. Those virgins who fear the opposite sex may express strong opinions about sexuality, may even be opposed to it and argue against it. But their arguments will sound like those of the bachelor uncle who sounds off about child-rearing.

I'm not saying that sexually-experienced people are superior to virgins. Neither are those experienced with spiritual power superior to those who are not. A person's first sexual experience may be of violent rape, and a rape victim is worse off for being "sexually experienced." There are some persons whose initial experience of the supernatural was a sort of spiritual rape by dark powers. In that case their whole view of supernatural power can be distorted.

Sex, both in its broadest and narrowest sense, is potent stuff. The experience of it is heady. It may make you obsessed with eroticism rather than with a spouse you love. This can lead to a sin-bound pursuit of the ultimate physical experience. Even where you know that loving your spouse is what matters, it can remain an evil thing. So long as you are pursuing the perfect relationship you remain an idolater.

Like sex, spiritual power is dangerously heady stuff. I remember praying with my wife for a two-year-old child in Malaysia. Her body was almost completely covered with raw, weeping eczematous areas. She ran around the room restlessly so that her parents had to catch her to bring her struggling to us. We began to pray and extended our hands to lay them on her. The instant our hands touched her she fell into profound and relaxed slumber in her parents' arms.

But there was more to follow. I shall never forget our sense of exhilaration and excitement as the weeping areas began to dry up, their borders shrinking visibly before our eyes like the shores of lakes in time of drought. That was power!

A person who has never experienced the impact of such a sight has no idea of its effect on one's emotions. People have been known to laugh and cry helplessly for hours after observing miraculous power, especially if the miracle is a major one touching someone close to them.

If you ever exercise spiritual power of that order, if you should ever see a congregation of hundreds weeping in broken repentance as you preach, the experience may make sexual love seem as banal as eating ice cream. Small wonder that Jesus needed to warn the seventy when they returned full of excitement after their successful mission. To be sure, he had seen Satan fall like lightning from heaven. Yes, indeed, he gave them even more authority and power. "However, do not rejoice that the spirits submit to you, but rejoice that your names are written in heaven" (Lk 10:20).

There is danger in power. Sexual power can make some men rapists and some women nymphomaniacs. Spiritual power can be equally destructive. There is therefore danger in every revival. We must be careful to hold to Christ's own scale of values.

Victims of Power

In chapter three I pointed out that manifestations offend some people and ensnare others. People who have never experienced the raw stuff may deny its reality or even attribute to Satan something the Holy Spirit has done. Those who have experienced the heady stuff may be lured in pursuit of power experiences. When that happens they are no different from a sex-obsessed person chasing the ultimate orgasm. To people like that, manifestations are a snare.

Divine power is holy power. People entrusted with it carry a heavy burden of responsibility. Those who reverence its source and realize the responsibility that comes with it, respect it. Others have exercised divine power and have displeased God by the way they did so. Did Moses eventually take spiritual power for granted? Why did he strike the rock in Kadesh? Was he merely being petulant? Or had familiarity with power bred contempt for holiness and for the word of the Lord? Moses certainly seemed to be upset, but the sentence pronounced against him was not for his petulance. God made the nature of Moses' offense clear. "Because you did not trust in me enough to honor me as holy . . . you will not bring this community into the land I give them" (Num 20:12).

Have you ever wondered why the sentence against Moses was so heavy? Who could have been more faithful, more devoted both to God and to Israel than Moses? What leader in human history has done more? Yet Moses was denied what might have been the crowning joy of his life. Why? God's word and God's power are holy and dangerous things. They can destroy those who handle them. Moses trusted God, but "not . . . enough to honor me as holy."

One prophet on whom mighty power rested lost his life before the mauling claws of a lion because he did not take the word of the Lord seriously enough (1 Kings 13:1-30). Uzzah, the son of Abinadab, did not handle power but did handle something very holy. He was killed at the threshing floor of Nacon, amid songs of worship and celebration, because he failed to realize the holiness of the God whose presence hovered over the ark of the covenant (2 Sam 6:1-8).

But notice carefully. Moses had done the will of God—at least in the sense that he had gathered elders and people as he had been instructed, and he had used supernatural power to supply water to the people. He had done the will of God with the power of God. Yet his heart had not been in fellowship with God. Jesus plainly teaches us that it is possible to do godly things with divine power but not have fellowship with God. "Many will say to me on that day, 'Lord, Lord, did we not prophesy in your name, and in your name drive out demons and perform many miracles?' Then will I tell them plainly, 'I never knew you. Away from me, you evil-doers!' " (Mt 7:22-23).

I do not understand why God gives more power to other people than he does to me. I resent it at times. But God has his own reasons, and my resentment is out of place. He is God and he knows what he is doing. Any of us can mishandle any gracious gift he bestows on us. Yet he never ceases to bestow.

Being sinful and weak, we can be clumsy in handling power and get into difficulties. But God does not take the same risks with us that the sorcerer took with his legendary apprentice. His purposes will never be frustrated, nor will his plans suffer from our bungling. But we may.

While Samson used spiritual power for some pretty sordid ends, God had his own purposes (Judg 14:4). Nevertheless Samson was hardly pleasing God by his childish rages, or by his dallying with Delilah. And while his use of power became a legend, he himself suffered greatly and needlessly.

Elijah's exercise of divine power makes for one of the most dramatic stories in Scripture. Through him God sent total drought, sent fire from heaven in the presence of many witnesses and then sent a storm of rain. What a sense of triumph he must have had!

But the ultimate effect of all this on Elijah was devastating. He sank into an appalling and suicidal depression. Why? We cannot be absolutely certain since Elijah does not tell us too much about what was going on inside him. But there are clues here and there in his subsequent interaction with God.

What we must not assume is that as a prophet he had a perfect knowledge of all future events. That would make him omniscient. It seems likely that he had his own scenario of what was to take place politically. Jezebel and her powerful influence seems to have been central to his thinking. He probably expected it to be overthrown. If so his view of his own role and his position (note 1 Kings 19:10) was unrealistic. This, combined with physical and emotional exhaustion, plunged him into a black vortex of terror and despair. He suffered because in his exercise of divine power he was not really in touch with God, and with what God was doing, even though he was a prophet.

We are dealing then with the problem of God's committing powers to men. It is evident that God places many good things in our power which can be wrongly and harmfully used. The sharper the knife, the greater its potential both for good and ill to ourselves and to others. We might expect God to have more concern for his own reputation than to entrust spiritual power to immature and imperfect men and women. But the fact is that he does.

Failing to understand this we feel that people who manifest God's power must be closer to him than others. But this is not necessarily so. Samson, as we have seen, was hardly a model of sanctity. We adopt a you-can't-have-it-both-ways mentality. Either the power is of God, and therefore the person exercising it must be pleasing to God, or else the person is displeasing God and the power (if it is real) must be from the pit. But miraculous power is never a reward for sanctity. God has been gracious enough all along to entrust it to sinful men and women who take him seriously but whose sanctity and doctrinal understanding is often less than ideal.

The Abuse of a Trust

Spiritual power committed to men leading revivals has grave dangers. The dramatic effects of the power are seductive and have misled men in a number of ways. Manifestations have been used to justify individuals and their particular theological views. They have contributed to pride and division among Christians. They have exposed leaders to the seduction of power and those who were led to the pursuit of subjective experiences for their own sake.

John Wesley justified his anti-Calvinist stance and his divisiveness by the manifestations in his meetings. It was unwise of him to do so for identical manifestations had been occurring under the ministry of the Erskines in Scotland, whose position, unlike Wesley's, was strongly Calvinistic, and Wesley was aware of this. In spite of this he saw the phenomena not only as a confirmation of his own calling, but as a sign of the correctness of his doctrine.

In a letter to his brother Charles dated June 23, 1739, he refers to his ordinary call (his ordination by a bishop) and his extraordinary call. Of the latter he writes, "My extraordinary call is witnessed by the work God doeth by my ministry; which prove that he is with me of a truth in this exercise of my office." Perhaps this might be expressed in another way: God bears witness in an extraordinary manner (through what Wesley was calling signs and wonders) that my thus exercising my ordinary call is pleasing in his sight.[1]

There is nothing wrong with this. But he goes further. His journal for Thursday April 23, 1739, records an incident in Bristol. It reads: "While I was preaching at Newgate, on these words, 'He that believeth hath everlasting life,' I was insensibly led, without any previous design, to declare strongly and explicitly, that God willeth 'all men to be' thus 'saved;' and to pray, that, 'if this were not the truth of God, he would not suffer the blind to go out of the way; but, if it were, he would bear witness to his word.' Immediately one, and another, and another sunk to the earth: They dropped on every side as thunderstruck. . . ."[2]

He requested similar divine confirmation on an almost identical doctrinal statement in the evening service the same day. Wesley was a godly man, greatly used of God. Why then should the journal entry disturb me?

There was controversy then, as now, about the issues of predestination and a limited atonement. Whitefield, who had entrusted the work in the Bristol area to Wesley, was aware that many of the Christians there were strong proponents of the Calvinist view and urged Wesley not to stir up controversy. It was in any case unnecessary to belabor the issue of a limited atonement. Hundreds were turning to the Lord in response to the preaching. That evening, however, he cast lots to determine whether he should continue the line of attack. The lot bade him, "print and preach."

Dallimore tells us: "But Wesley had already been preparing a sermon in readiness for such directions. Accordingly, having received the directions he finished it and, despite the warnings he had been given by his friends, on the following Sunday morning he preached it. . . . Strange to say it was but four weeks to the day since Whitefield had trustingly introduced him to his Bristol people on this same spot, having 'conjured' him not to do the very thing he was now doing!"[3] Wesley was using the manifestations to justify his betrayal of a trust. That betrayal was apparently not as spontaneous as he claims. Rather it appears to have been premeditated.

From that day revival forces were divided, and though attempts at reconciliation were made, the healing was never complete. The repercussions from the division are with us to this day. Blame is irrelevant. The error that must be addressed concerns the significance of manifestations occurring in Wesley's meetings. And in criticizing that error I have no wish to minimize John Wesley's greatness, but rather to state that his greatness has nothing to do with the signs and wonders in his meetings, and that it is unfortunate that like Elijah, his view of matters was distorted by them. A manifestation of power is not a sign of God's special approval of one's person or of one's theology, nor does it validate one's assessment of a national situation. God is grieved by our party spiritedness and does not bestow power to prove one group right and another wrong.

John Cennick, troubled by Wesley's tendency to foster the manifestations for the wrong reasons wrote:

At first no one knew what to say, but it was soon called the pangs of the new birth, the work of the Holy Ghost, casting out the old man, etc., but some were offended and left the Societies entirely when they saw Mr. Wesley encourage it. I often doubted it was not of the enemy when I saw it, and disputed with Mr. Wesley for calling it the work of God; but he was strengthened in his opinion after he had wrote about it to Mr. Erskine in Scotland, and had received a favorable answer. And frequently when none were agitated in the meetings, he prayed, Lord! where are thy tokens and signs, and I don't remember ever to have seen it otherwise than that on his so praying several were seized and screamed out.[4]

Cennick was not alone in being troubled and confused. Whether the power of God accounted for these (as distinct from former) manifestations I cannot say. But I know the enemy delights to mimic the work of God and to sow confusion among his followers. His actions nearly destroyed Cennick's usefulness.

Harmful Excesses

John Cennick's phrase, "all manner of fancies,"[5] aptly describes the strange variety of harmful excesses that have always been a side effect, an undesirable and damaging consequence, of what God's Spirit may do in an individual. Some people believe it to be impossible that the power of the Holy Spirit could have unholy consequences in an individual's life. But it can.

The work of the Holy Spirit, Edwards saw, could be an "accidental occasion" of sin.[6] By this he meant a means or a cause, not a necessary means, but a possible or secondary means. He saw that a few unstable people who were touched by God's power were led into strange errors. His critics, observing this, condemned the revival movement, seeing it as a work of Satan. The strange results, may have indeed been of Satan, like the strange fire offered in the wilderness, but the movement as a whole was of God.

The excitement of power, of visions, of touching the fringes of a new dimension intoxicate the unstable and the unwary. Judgment goes by the board. And in the absence of good pastoral oversight, harmful excess follows. The mainstream of a revival movement corrects its errors as it goes along. Power for holy living becomes more important than power for dramatic jerkings. But in the early stages, the sight of powerful manifestations proves seductive, and so a sort of lunatic fringe develops along with the mainstream. My own feeling is that the proportion of false manifestations increases progressively the more time elapses, as certain segments of the movement see them as guaranteeing that they remain at the core and that their members alone are the authentically revived.

Paul the apostle was the subject of extraordinary spiritual experiences, and God was merciful to him. Because of the abundance of his revelations he was given a "thorn in the flesh," lest he should be "exalted above measure." Who knows what damage he might have caused in the Gentile church if the astounding revelations made to him had gone to his head and seriously impaired his judgment.

If Edwards is right, there is a sense in which divine power can be an occasion of corruption. The effect in this case tells us nothing about the sanctity of the cause. And if divine power can be an occasion of corruption, we may say that a great amount of divine power can, by being wrongly used, be an occasion of great corruption. Was this not the case with Lucifer to whom so much of it was entrusted?

Christian leaders who know something of revival power—beware! Use that power. It was given you to use. But tremble as you use it. Remember its holy origin. Beware of playing the big shot.

And above all beware of calling on that power in order to reassure yourself that you still have it.

Early in 1985 I made the acquaintance of a Vineyard pastor for whom I have profound respect. He struck me as being straightforward, honest and humble. He also knows something of spiritual power. On two occasions he requested the evidence of the Holy Spirit's work. On the first occasion within a minute or two many people in the room were obviously affected. Though I did not have the opportunity of interviewing people personally, I had little doubt about the genuineness of what was happening, and could only thank God for it.

But the second occasion was different. Again there were power manifestations, but this time I was troubled. I could not place my finger on what was wrong. I had an inner suspicion that the pastor had an emotional need to see God working supernaturally again and that his own need had motivated his "calling down the Spirit." My criticism had no real foundation. I had only the vaguest subjective impression to go on. Could it be that he was repeating John Wesley's error?

A couple of nights later, even though I am not subject to this sort of dream, I dreamed vividly. I saw a couple of people setting up a new flag post outside the church. All we had to do was to plant the flagpole into a sort of tube set in a circular cement base. But as I stared at the tube, I saw it was both too narrow, too fragile and not truly vertical. Moreover, the cement base was too small and shallow for the large and heavy flag post it was to support. I turned to my helpers and told them we would have to break up the foundation and replace it with a more substantial one, making sure that this time the socket for the flag post was big enough, strong enough and truly vertical.

I woke with the following words drumming through my mind, "Thou hast given a banner to them that fear thee, because of the truth."

In my mind the flag and the flag post symbolized the church's public testimony, that which was displayed. It was crucial that the display reflected God's truth. I thought about the church and the second time that the leader exercised spiritual power. Did that display truly reflect what the kingdom was about? I called the leader, described my dream, and told him of my fears. He listened without being defensive and promised to think about the matter.

A year later I saw him again, and he asked me to go into his office to talk. He thanked me for what I had said a year before and told me that God had shown him that his motivation had indeed been subtly awry on the occasion I had mentioned. He had observed the same thing in another brother and this had brought home to him his own danger. "It would eventually have destroyed my ministry if it had gone on," he said.

Sinning Servants Who Are "Mightily Used"

Even Jesus was accused by religious critics of using miraculous power with a demonic source. The same accusation has been leveled at almost all revivals. (It seems to be a rule of thumb—if you don't like what is happening but cannot explain it easily, then say it is of the devil.) In the next chapter we will look more carefully at demonic miracles and how they can be distinguished from a work of the Spirit of God. But the incident I have just described really has to do with something else—what I might call the demonization of power; that is, using power the way demons do.

All power in heaven, in earth—or anywhere else that might exist—is God's. He is the sole source of all varieties of power. All belongs by right to him and to him alone. It never ceases to be his by right. But God seems to delegate power.

I must be careful at this point, for I am not a theologian. And the very statement, "God seems to delegate power," would be contested hotly by some who are far more expert than I. Really we are dealing with mysteries which defy human understanding. Perhaps it might be better to say that human decisions have a bearing on the immediate effects of some forms of power.

Delegated power, if we can use such a term, remains God's power, but angels and humans appear to be given at times a sort of "power of attorney" over it. They become entrusted servants using that power in accordance with the mandates God gave them. But because humans and angels can be rebellious and do what they want rather than what God wants, they may use power wrongly.

We can abuse power that rightly belongs to God. Certainly we can abuse physical power. What terrible things we have done with power in the course of history! We use power to kill, to maim, to exploit, to corrupt and to incite depravity. For instance, we use electronic power to deprave, employing it to promote pornography, violence and human degradation. Our abuse of physical power achieved its hideous apex in our crucifixion of God the Son. And the fact that he was crucified according to the "set purpose and foreknowledge of God" in no way mitigates the horrendous nature of the crime—the crime of the demonization of power.

But you may say, "So much for physical power. But surely spiritual power is different. God grants spiritual power as we walk close to him, as we pray, read Scripture, seek to be obedient in all things."

No, it doesn't quite work like that. Power is not a reward for holiness—a kind of spiritual merit badge. Samson's power seemed to depend not on his lifestyle but on his haircuts—or rather the absence of them. You say, "Yes, but that was obedience, wasn't it?" Of course, it was. But long hair did not make Samson holy, except in a symbolic sense. It marked him as one set apart. After all, every Christian is a "set apart" person. But that is just my point. Like Samson, Christians who fail to live holy lives sometimes exercise divine power. Or so it appears from the godly fruit they produce.

Samson made use of divinely given strength to have sex with Philistine women and get away with it. Admittedly God used these incidents for purposes of his own. The book of Judges emphasizes the fact that God has purposes that even the weaknesses of his servants automatically feed into. But are we to understand that in order to effect his purposes and plans, God didn't care how Samson went about the business? didn't care about him playing games with enemy prostitutes?

No, Samson sinned. God abhorred it. But God perpetually uses the sins of the sinful to effect his holy purposes. It is a way of defeating the devil. Sin is rebellion, and rebellion against God never works. It cannot work because God takes the results of the evil we have brought into being and transforms them into greater good. Rebellion will never damage him. But he is not the author of the sins or the evil.

I am convinced that God still delegates miraculous power and that it can still be abused. Some twentieth-century healers are like an empowered Samson, but a Samson wrongly using power. Some churches are guilty of exaggerated reports, loose morals and a use of divine power for self-promotion and aggrandizement.

But the power is divine power. The work represents neither fraud nor a display of demonic influence. The healers are abusing their gifts and calling. If they are deceived, and some of them seem to be, the deception is not one in which demons fool them into thinking they are using divine power when in fact the source is demonic.

Rather, God gives them power, just as he did to Samson. But fascinated with a very exciting game, they allow themselves to be deceived by believing they are still pleasing God and enjoying fellowship with him simply because they are surrounded by enthusiasm and results. Results prove only that the power is real. The fact that the power of many delinquent healers comes from God lies in the fact that untold numbers of lives are redeemed through their ministry. God fulfills his own purposes. His loving heart is satisfied.

But the results prove nothing about the character or holiness of the person who wields the power. Results do not mean that he is pleasing God or, on the other hand, that he was tricked into using the devil's power.

Power is given as God chooses, to whom God chooses, in the measure God chooses. And while he often chooses to withdraw it from a sinning servant, his purpose in so doing is to teach the lesson of Ai.

When the Israelites defeated Jericho, they were given strict instructions to set aside all gold, silver, bronze and iron for the Lord's treasury (Josh 6:18-19). Individuals were not to take these spoils for their personal possessions. But one man did, Achan. The result? When Israel next did battle with the city of Ai, Israel was defeated. Joshua then cried to the Lord and discovered the defeat was due to the sin among the people. Once Joshua and the people punished Achan, Israel then conquered Ai (Josh 7—8).

The point is not merely that disobedience leads to defeat, and certainly not that holiness leads to power. Rather it is that holiness is necessary if we want ongoing fellowship with God. God wanted fellowship with his people. On that occasion he allowed them to suffer defeat because he had been trying to impress on them his longing to have them walk in fellowship with him. That is why God uses any painful means to get at us—because he wants our fellowship.

Churches are slowly getting used to the fact that this or that Christian leader, who "was being tremendously used by God," was all along involved in secret sins of one sort or another. While the sin is upsetting, it is even more disturbing to us that "God continued to use" the person. (The fact is that the leader was not "being used by" God at all. If anything he was using God—or at least God's power. And that was where his or her deepest sin lay rather than in the sordid things done when the heart was out of tune with God's.)

The phrase "used by God" can be religious cant. It was originally a way of attributing the glory to God. We were embarrassed about spiritual power, mistakenly supposing it to be a badge of sanctity rather than a practical tool of service. Satan has used this mistaken concept to blind us to the horrors we can commit with the holy things God trusts us with. It also blinds those who misuse power to the nature of sin and to the fact that they may, if they continue, fall into the hands of Satan and be yet more grossly deceived by him. We shall look at examples of this in the next chapter.

We are capable of defiling power. In so doing we desecrate the most holy things. It does no good to pretend that we cannot. We can abuse the gifts and privileges we are given. To abuse any power is sin. But to abuse the holy powers closest to God's person is horrendous sin. And we do it all the time.

The One-Club Golfer

So far we have looked at more than one danger inherent in being entrusted with spiritual power. We may allow ourselves to be seduced by its exciting nature into pursuing it as an end in itself. Or we may forget the holiness of its source and use it carelessly and out of fellowship with God. We may feel it validates our personal ministry, our assessment of a situation and even our doctrinal views. But it has common, practical dangers.

A golfer who used only one club would not get very far. Though most golfers favor certain clubs over others, the better the golfer, the wider the variety of the clubs he or she uses. The same is true in any sport or profession. The better the athlete or professional, the wider the variety of techniques or instruments employed.

The same principle holds in matters of the kingdom. God has equipped the church with certain "clubs," those responsibilities and powers given for the church's ministry and for her own health. They all involve the powers of the world to come. God has equipped her with the holy Scriptures, the marvelous privilege of prayer, with worship, with the sacraments of baptism and the breaking of bread, with the keys of corporate fellowship and discipline and with anointings and giftings of the Holy Spirit. They are notes that should blend together harmoniously in the church's life and ministry. Balance involves the incorporation of all.

Wesley, certainly for one period of his life, had an imbalanced dependency on "supernatural" manifestations. Happily it neither impeded his evangelism nor led to the neglect of discipline, worship or the sacraments in the church's life. Most Christian leaders, whether they go in for "signs and wonders" or not, avoid a one-club approach. The problem occurs more commonly with rank and file members of churches.

People who have been converted in a ministry where powerful manifestations of the Spirit occur are understandably and rightly impressed by them. But unless their training and discipline teaches them to be just as impressed with other "clubs," and in particular with the skills of investigating Scripture for themselves, they will use their one club excessively and inappropriately, in circumstances where the real need may be for others.

Current renewal movements are characterized by a new discovery of the joy of worship and the availability of divine power. I have noticed that in many smaller home and kinship groups that while lip service is paid both to the importance of studying Scripture and of intercessory prayer, nobody does either in such gatherings. The time is devoted to singing songs of worship and to mutual prayer support. Both of these are necessary, but they are no substitute for the others. In some groups nobody brings Bibles. And having conversed with many of the people I find that few people know how to study it. (But this, if I am to be fair, is a problem common to churches where renewal is looked down on, where Scripture is the major "club." In such churches, too, lip service is paid to Bible study. But the members are spoon-fed. Most lack Bible study skills.)

This must change if renewal movements (and also nonrenewal movements) are to fulfill what God intends for his people. One-club golfers cannot play a well-rounded game. A driver is not helpful either in a bunker or in the rough. One may pray over a fellow Christian in the power of the Spirit, but the prayer will not make that person mature. Even a genuine release from impediments to maturity will not impart Bible knowledge nor even the skills for acquiring it. It will only impart a hunger for Scripture. Similarly, one may study Scripture until the whole Bible is memorized and yet know nothing either of power over sin or power for service.

Dread That Debilitates

Yet my main theme has to do with the church's panicky flight at the approach of revival, and the failure to recognize it when God sends it. Revival has dangers. But our fear may lead us to reject what God sends. We must not neglect power because it has dangers.

The greatest fear in some quarters is that what appears to be the power of God may be nothing more than a massive hoax by the enemy. It is a fear that is paralyzing whole segments of the church, a dread that debilitates, that causes our hands to hang slack and our feet to lag at a time when the trumpet calls for advance and attack. I shall examine this fear in the next chapter.

10
Stolen Power

SNAKE AND SERAPH ABIDE THERE SIDE BY
side. . . ." WILLIAM JAMES
"We must observe, therefore, that . . . in proportion as God is guiding
the soul and communicating with it, he gives the devil leave to act with
it after this manner." JOHN OF THE CROSS

In the previous chapter we looked at the danger of spiritual
power. It is a danger that may make us avoid manifestations of it
altogether. But if we back away fearfully we may limit our effectiveness in the battle that is important to all of us. Fear can paralyze.
And in this case it takes on one of two forms—a fear of anything
subjective, and a related fear of being deceived by the powers of
darkness. Some of my friends view the kinds of things I have been

describing as unhealthily subjective. Others believe they may have a diabolical source.

In this chapter we shall both look at the role of subjective experiences in our walk with Christ, and also examine the danger of Satanic deception.

A Tribute to the Devil

Some Christians who fear experience disproportionately attach more credence to accounts of occult power than to accounts of divine power. I am not altogether sure how to account for this, except to wonder whether the condition does not represent a major triumph of the adversary. A friend of mine who is a Bible scholar related the following story to a colleague of his who viewed contemporary miracles skeptically.

"A Christian young woman with a two-inch discrepancy in the length of her legs (a discrepancy that called for the wearing of special shoes) was delighted to be healed by an occult healer. Unfortunately depressions and other distress followed. Eventually she confessed what she had done to her pastor and renounced her sin. At once the depression left and the difference in the length of her legs returned. Once again she had to have special shoes built."

Remarkably, the colleague was impressed. Was he paying an unwitting tribute to demonic power, of a kind that he was unwilling to give to God? Do we live in a world where the devil can flaunt his miracles before the powerless kingdom of Christ? Ironically we are sending missionaries to equip Third World Christians to face the hordes of darkness and their powers while stripping them of many of their weapons of war. When our confidence in our interpretation of Scripture takes us to such a position it needs to be reexamined.

Not to have experienced the power of God is to be spiritually naive and an easier target for demonic deception. We need to know both, the one by the grace of God, the other in its malignant opposition to us.

But let us make no mistake about the reality of Satanic power today.

There are many contemporary accounts of miraculous demonic powers. Among the Family of Love movement, once known as the Children of God, are documented healings, along with false spiritual gifts such as tongues and prophecy. The source of many of them was diabolical. In her book *The Children of God*, Deborah Davis (formerly Linda Berg, daughter of Moses David Berg, the founder of the movement) gives her father's colorful description of how at the age of fifty he received something he had longed for all his life—the gift of tongues.

"I was lying there between Martha and Maria [his illicit wives] praying like a house afire, and all of a sudden before I even knew what happened I was praying in tongues. . . . It was probably Abrahim. I was finally desperate enough to let the Lord really take over and take control. Abrahim was praying through me in the Spirit."[1]

Abrahim was a spirit guide Berg had picked up at a Gypsy camp, reputedly the spirit of a former Gypsy king. At that point, if not before then, dark powers had invaded the movement called the Children of God, and iniquity was soon to abound more and more. Pride and fear had opened the movement to deception. It was prepared neither spiritually nor intellectually to distinguish between dark powers and divine.

Ice and Fire

Let us be clear about matters. The powers of darkness are real and active. They can and do work miracles. Not all the witches and warlocks interviewed on TV are phony. In modern Japan people flock to the centers of new religious cults where spectacular miracles fascinate them. Earlier we were reminded how the Egyptian magicians in Moses' day were able to turn their rods into serpents and water into blood. To a certain point they were able to imitate what Aaron did. But their powers were inferior. Aaron's serpent swallowed the serpents the magicians had conjured up. Moreover, the magicians seemed unable to undo the evil they had done. They could not turn blood back into water.

But Pharaoh, looking at a prophet in his day, made the mistake some skeptics make today when they look at the working of God's power. Pharaoh saw divine power as mere magic. He believed that Moses was another magician, not a prophet of God, and that Moses and his own magicians were all of a piece—simple workers of magic. Pharaoh had seen the finger of God, but did not know what he had seen.

Jesus referred to that finger in Luke's Gospel. Once again, the context has to do with the extreme importance of never attributing God's work to Satan, of never confusing the work of the two clashing kingdoms. Accused of casting demons out by the authority of their prince, Jesus protested the absurdity of such a notion, making it clear that demons can be cast out only by "the finger of God," and that wherever we see the finger of God, we also see a manifestation of the kingdom of God (Lk 11:20).

Now why should there be any danger of mistaking the finger of God for the horns of the devil? On the face of it the notion seems absurd. How could such dissimilar sources give rise to similar products?

There is one source of supernatural power, and one only. Satan's power is power once entrusted to him by God. God was the Creator of the power just as, being the Creator of all that is, he created Satan himself. The power was meant for use in God's service. It is what we might call embezzled power. And that is exactly what magic is—stolen power, used for the user's delight. Whenever anyone, Christian or non-Christian, angel or demon, uses power for selfish ends (for the love of power or for the justification or glory of the self), the power can be called magical power. It is the same power with the same characteristics put to a wrong use and subtly changed by that use. Christians who use God's power in this way have begun to act like sorcerers. Angels so using it fall.

Because magic is power that was originally created by God, it will always act like divine power in many respects. Its outward characteristics will not distinguish it from godly power. One cannot distinguish divine power from Satanic power by merely comparing certain features of both.

To be sure, there are differences. There are not only objective tests but subjective ones. Those who know both can perceive them. A spiritist medium converted under the preaching of Martyn Lloyd-Jones in Wales during a time of spiritual quickening, described her experience to the friend who had brought her.

"The moment I entered your chapel and sat down on a seat amongst the people, I was conscious of a supernatural power. I was conscious of the same sort of supernatural power as I was accustomed to in our spiritist meetings, but there was one big difference; I had a feeling that the power in your chapel was a clean power."[2]

The woman knew spiritual power subjectively. She was conscious of it in a way that few modern Christians are. She had never experienced power except from an evil source until she entered that chapel where the Holy Spirit was working in revival power. For her the experience had two layers. Intellectually and objectively she had looked at truth. And in her spirit she was aware of power—the same power yet different, different because it was clean.

She states that the supernatural power of which she was conscious was "the same sort of supernatural power as I was accustomed to in our spiritist meetings." Precisely. As power, it had the same source. Polluted water is still water. It may look like, behave like, and feel like pure water. The two may seem indistinguishable at times. However, polluted water can in many cases be detected by its taste. Polluted spiritual power always can—by those who have learned to "taste" in the spirit.

Subjective learning must never take place apart from a close walk with the Lord and an ongoing study of Scripture. The subjective and the objective are meant to go hand in hand. But the subjective is meant to begin early in the Christian life and not to be only for "advanced" saints. Children must learn early the difference between the comfort of warmth and the heat that burns. They learn it first by feel and by the guidance of their elders, and only later by an intellectual grasp of thermodynamics.

The genuineness of the former spiritist's spiritual perception can be understood by another reaction she had. Years later in a Bible class for women led by Mrs. Lloyd-Jones, the woman was asked what she thought of Saul, Samuel and the Witch of Endor. Hanging her head she said she "preferred never to think of such evil any more."[3]

True revulsion to Satanic power can only arise from experience of it.

Early in 1984 I elected to spend a week or so in fasting and prayer as I sought God's guidance about how to spend the last years of my life. One day as I knelt by my bedside, I had the powerful impression that God was present and that he was asking me questions. At least I thought it was God.

"Are you willing to obey me even if it means losing all your friends?"

Anxiety gripped me. The thought of losing friends was very painful. I said, "Yes, Lord—at least I want to even if . . ."

"Will you be willing to follow me through persecution? What about going to prison?"

I grew sick with fear. Determinedly I said, "Yes."

"Will you remain faithful, even if you are tortured?"

Strength seemed to ebb out of me. I was slumped over the edge of the bed, trembling. "I hope so, Lord. But I'd need your grace. I could so easily deny you." I am a coward. I saw my cowardice and hated it. I felt only contempt for the pitiful offering I had brought to God. The room seemed to be growing darker. The colors were fading on the bedcovers and curtains.

"Would you be willing to die for me?"

Mentally I said, "Yes." I slid backward from the bed and slumped on the carpet, filled with terror and self-loathing—loathing that I should be so weak. With a clarity I had never before known I saw my corruption and sin and was sickened by it. I lost any clear sense of time and began to groan aloud, each groan affording a moment's relief from the weight of terror that seemed to be crushing my body. By now I was lying flat on my back. It was an effort to breathe. Remembering textbook descriptions of the early signs of some forms of insanity, I began to wonder if I was going mad.

In time, and little by little, I began to experience a degree of relief. I was able to stop groaning and soon after to stand. I was still surrounded by a strange darkness, and though I could see clearly enough and could have named any color you might have pointed to, all colors were darkly colorless (contradictory as this may sound). Then I began to worry about my wife. Had she heard me groaning? Would she be upset?

Those fears were groundless. In the living room I found myself alone and stood musing, a mantle of dread still hanging heavily on my shoulders. Then in a flash, almost as though a switch had been flipped, the fear and the darkness were gone. Instantaneously colors were colors again. I was myself, sane, cheerful, but puzzled as to what had happened.

"Do you know what I have been doing to you?" The words were clear and powerful, though in my mind rather than in my ears. I made no reply. "I have allowed you to be in the hands of Satan for a while." So that was it! It had not been God facing me with a challenge, even though the sense of supernatural power had been about me. It had been an enemy, accusing and terrifying. But why had it happened?

"I wanted you to know the difference between his fear and mine." Then I understood. I knew exactly what he was talking about. For during the previous eighteen years I had "seen" the Lord three times. On each occasion I had been overcome with terror. But the terror I had just experienced and the terror of seeing a manifestation of God were overwhelmingly different. I would be less afraid of confusing them in future. The subjective awareness of the two, so very different, yet so similar in their supernaturalness and their power, had been burned into my bones and the cells of my body.

The difference was the difference between dry ice and fire. Both can burn to the touch. But while ice preserves corruption, fire purges corruption and burns away dross. Fire purifies. Fire is clean.

Imagery, Revelation and Deception

Nowhere are the similarities between divine power and demonic more apparent than in the matter of dreams, visions and the imagery common to both. The only imagery presented to us in Scripture is the imagery through which God speaks. It abounds in the writings of the prophets, in their dreams and in their visions. The book of Revelation consists of image piled on image.

But we have already seen that Satan imitates God. If God speaks through imagery, Satan does too. God communicates powerful truth through imagery. Satan uses imagery to deceive and ensnare. Therefore, a vision may be a saving call from heaven or a treacherous lure from hell. It can be an agent of deliverance, or it can forge chains of bondage.

Many of us, influenced more than we realize by the prevailing naturalism and humanism that molds so much of our thinking, conclude that dreams and visions are for emotionally disturbed people. Others, aware of the use of imagery by the powers of darkness, condemn anybody who has anything to do with imagery. Yet whether we like it or not, none of us can even think without employing imagery. Our brains function in such a way that we are dependant on visual, sensory and even auditory imagery. It floods our consciousness when we dream, and colors our fantasies when we wake. Memory is primarily a matter of imagery.

There is, of course, a verbal component in our stream of consciousness. But it is only one component of several. When we "listen" to the stream of our thoughts, we hear not only words, but the sound of words or the sight of them. We "see" people's faces when we think about them, and if we don't see them we are troubled. We say, "I can't call her face to mind, somehow."

Imagery comes from our stored memories. Wilder Penfield startled the world of neurology some years ago by his discovery that an electrode inserted into the right temporal lobe of a patient could conjure up, when stimulated, a video replay of events in the subject's past. Sights, sounds, smells and feelings would all recur, so that the subject would say, "I had forgotten—I had forgotten all about it . . ." Every detail would be present, stored in the brain in the condensed form, not of a long verbal description, but of the original event. When the electrical stimulus was discontinued, the replay would cease.

If it was restarted, the video would continue from the point it left off. The patient would relive a memory, seeing the same sights, hearing the same sounds, experiencing the same feelings over again.

Our minds are like video-stereo systems with antennae that can receive messages from beyond—the good and the evil beyond. The beyond communicates largely using the words and images already stored in our memories. But at the Fall something happened to us. Reception was no longer clear. Tuning was damaged. A need arose for written records dealing with the essentials of the beyond. Over the course of millennia that record was compiled, as people whose tuning may have been a little better were charged with important transmissions. We call them the prophets.

But humans have never stopped receiving communications from the beyond. It is just that the communications from God were never meant to supplant the written communication, which remains paramount. Knowing it will help us not to be deceived. However, to say that Scripture renders dreams and visions obsolete is not true. As the Sandfords put it, "That would be the same as saying to a general in battle, 'We need not respond to your couriers; we have the original battle plans, drawn up before the war began!' "[4]

Yet I have always been cautious about subjective guidance, particularly in the form of visions. And I can certainly appreciate the terrible fears of some people nowadays who have been "raped" by the powers of darkness. Such a person's fear of visual imagery may be particularly strong.[5]

Deborah (Linda Berg) Davis in *The Children of God* struggles to answer the question of how something which began as an evangelistic work among hippies, could have evolved slowly into one of the most iniquitous and demonic movements of the twentieth century. Perhaps we shall never know the answer fully. But certainly excessive pride, hunger for power and contempt for other believers and Christian groups opened the way to personal sexual sin, and later to the search for a spirit guide. At some point along the way, powers of darkness progressively took over the movement.

The case of Jim Jones is less clear. Was he at any point a believer? It is hard to be sure. Certainly he knew extraordinary spiritual power, the source of which is by no means clear. But as I watched a video of him on one occasion I heard him proclaim a healing "in the name of Jesus, of Jehovah and of all the world's great religions"—hardly a Christian proclamation.

In *The Fight* I pointed out that dreams and visions in Scripture seemed to be given principally to people who were stubborn and needed to be shaken (like Peter with his attitude to Gentiles, and Saul of Tarsus over his attitude to Christians) or on occasions when the nature of the communication was extraordinary and incredible (such as to the Virgin Mary).

I was and still am, concerned about subjective guidance becoming a substitute for a knowledge of Scripture. Immature and unstable people get into trouble with visions. Yet I cannot and must not deny that they occur, and that they are occurring with increasing frequency to many people. And their source is sometimes divine and sometimes demonic.

How then can we tell (whether we are dealing specifically with imagery or with manifestations in general) what is from God, and what is of self or of Satan? Subjective knowing is not enough. What objective tests can we apply?

The Proof of the Pudding

First, we must shun generalizations. We cannot say that manifestations are good because of this, or that visions are of the devil because of that. As we have seen already, what God does, the enemy mimics, and can mimic superbly. Therefore, it is wrong and dangerous to attribute to God the work of Satan (Mt 12:31-32).

Pharisees in every age have played the role of witch hunters. They did so in Jesus' day, and they do so now. When they accused Jesus of using Satanic power he stated a principle which is valid in every age: ". . . A tree is recognized by its fruit" (Mt 12:33). If we see good fruit follow the manifestations in someone's life, we must assume that the source was good. We judge visions by what they lead to. God has his aims, and the devil has his. The aims are utterly different. Therefore, the results of their actions will differ *morally and spiritually.*

The Holy Spirit will not deceive. His weapon is always truth and enlightenment. He will lead in the direction of holiness. Satan blinds (2 Cor 4:4). As an angel of light the devil even uses visions to deceive and ensnare. He will draw us slowly into sin and unbelief. Therefore, we must judge any manifestation, be it in the form of a vision or of an outburst of weeping, by its fruits. We must judge an expression of emotion by what it leads to. If bitter tears lead to a holier walk, then we may be sure the Holy Spirit produced the weeping.

Second, we must be very cautious about judging by specific features of a manifestation or vision. If Satan can appear as an angel of light, then details can be seriously misleading. On the other hand, something that has for us an evil association may not necessarily imply that an evil work is going on.

Patti Blue told me the following story about her grandfather, Donald McCullough (father of Pastor John McCullough of Seattle,

Washington). She had checked the details carefully with surviving relatives.

Donald McCullough had been a homesteader in Montana who in the early 1920's moved with his family down to California and bought a couple of ten-acre farms near Porterfield. McCullough was described as a "godless, foul-mouthed" man, who when invited by the local pastor to teach a Sunday-school class in the community asked his wife, "What does he think I could teach them? To curse and play cards?"

McCullough's wife was converted at a tent meeting in the community to which she had persuaded her husband to take her. He seemed to tolerate her attraction to a Pentecostal form of Christianity but showed no personal interest, and his wife forbore to press him. One hot summer day on the back porch of his home, his wife was startled to observe his extreme agitation. He appeared to be struggling against a profound conviction of sin. She heard him say, "God, what I want is a religion like Mormonism or Russelism so as I can do as I please and go to heaven anyhow."

The exact sequence of events is unclear. At one point she observed him on the floor of the porch, rolling and beating the ground with his arms and legs. A stream of unremitting curses fell from his lips. She had the wisdom to leave him there, sensing that his battle, which lasted for several hours, was with God.

The next morning he was a changed man. He was never again heard to swear, and he lost a compulsion to smoke. He developed a hunger for Scripture and prayed much. Some time later he became an evangelist and church planter, preaching widely and indefatigably throughout California, Idaho and Montana.

McCullough's conversion must be judged by its fruits, not by the nature of the manifestation associated with it, which hardly commends itself.

Jonathan Edwards gave five signs that determine whether a work is or is not the work of the Holy Spirit. They form part of an exposition of 1 John 4, which according to Edwards must deal both with rules and fact—rules from the passage he was expounding, and facts from the careful observation of manifestations or the examination of reliable reports. All the rules (which are summarized as follows) have to do with the eventual effects of the work in the person's life, which should be—

1. Giving more honor to the historic Jesus, the Son of God and the Savior of the world;

2. Opposing Satan's kingdom by discouraging sin, lust and the world (the lust of the flesh, of the eyes, plus the pride of life);

3. Holding Scripture in high esteem;

4. Increasingly realizing that life is short, that there is another world, that they have immortal souls and must give an account of themselves to God, that they are sinful by nature and practice, and that they are helpless to overcome this without Christ; and

5. Expressing love for Christ and for others, especially toward fellow Christians which should not be characterized by hostility.

Edwards points out that you can be more certain that the work is not some sort of delusion when it is observed in many people, of many different types, in various places, than when it is only seen in a few places among a few people who know each other well. His point is not that the size of a movement matters. Instead, if the outbreaks occur in widely scattered areas, the chances of a sort of infection are minimized. He agrees that ideological fashions could account for beliefs, but the more widespread and varied it is, the more seriously it must be taken.[6]

The Dread That Dismays

Anyone who has caught a glimpse of the cosmic battle in which we are involved will be stunned and terrified. And anyone who has seen or been involved in displays of demonic power is also filled with fear. Our particular nightmares have to do with the power and the deceptions of the enemy. We feel helpless before the skill and the might of so formidable an adversary. Even to view the battle itself, the battle in the heavenlies, to see the hordes of darkness, and to hear angelic trumpetings above the thunder of battle, is to quake with dread at one's pitiful smallness and vulnerability.

Yet Scripture calls us to be strong and courageous. We are to "be strong in the Lord and in his mighty power" (Eph 6:10). We must not fear to pick up and wield weapons that are not of this world, weapons charged with divine potency, weapons that destroy the Lie (2 Cor 10:4-5). Above all, we must beware the temptation to run and hide from unaccustomed situations, to cling to the imagined safety of the familiar and "normal."

The fear of the powers of darkness is commonly unconscious, motivating our postures and attitudes without our realizing what is happening. A pastor in New York with whom I recently had lunch told me in the course of conversation that he had no fear of Satan or of the occult. Trained in a well-known seminary, he was knowledgeable and experienced, and for years had engaged in an effective counseling ministry with demonized persons.

At the time, however, his own church was passing through a crisis, a crisis that demanded that he make a personal decision about the nature of certain supernatural manifestations which had begun to occur in the church. The Holy Spirit must have been working, since without my saying anything he suddenly corrected his statement.

"You know I *am* afraid," he said. "I've never realized it before, but I'm held back by a fear of being deceived by Satan. It paralyzes me from taking a stand one way or the other." Fear was holding him back both from knowing and from action.

He asked me to pray for him, and as we prayed the Holy Spirit continued to work powerfully, so that he was stunned by the sudden opening of his mind and heart to realities he had kept at bay for years.

Is Worldwide Revival Possible?
For the last few years the church in some areas has been expanding

rapidly while in the hearts of Christians the kingdom seems to have been losing ground. "Religion is growing in importance among Americans but morality is losing ground. . . . There is very little difference in the behavior of the churched and the unchurched on a wide range of items including lying, cheating, and pilferage," writes George Gallup.[7] The advance of the kingdom of God does not always coincide with our evangelistic efforts.

Kingdom advances can never be measured statistically. Yet wherever local churches are proliferating and church membership goes on increasing, we should suspect that the kingdom may be advancing. Precisely this is happening in several areas of the Third World. In Latin America (particularly in Chile, Argentina, Brazil and Colombia) there has been an explosion of church growth over the last twenty-five years. The same is true of Africa.

Most remarkable of all have been events in mainland China. In 1984 I visited the Centre for Chinese Church Research in Kowloon Tong, Hong Kong. There I learned that in a largely hostile environment between 1980 and 1984 an explosive advance of Christianity was bothering the government in Peking. Four research reports on China gave conversion estimates ranging between 25 million and 100 million during that five-year period. The advance had proliferated among unofficial house churches. No overseas denomination, no evangelistic or missionary effort could be held responsible for the explosion, though missionary broadcasts had certainly helped. It was something God was doing.

The movement was not without error and problems. Leadership was often persecuted. Consequently there were almost no experienced leaders and a grossly inadequate supply of Bibles. Erroneous practices occurred in some areas. Yet seasoned China-watchers were in agreement that the movement was of the Holy Spirit. Moreover, the rapidity of the development worried the Peking government who feared that if its expansion were not checked, social problems similar to those caused by the Polish Solidarity could arise.

Thus from Africa, Latin America and China come reports which seem to suggest unparalleled advances in Christ's kingdom. From these areas also come reports of "hysterical behavior." In themselves they are not particularly important. But let there be no mistake about why I focus on them. They indicate more a phase of the battle than of the spiritual state of those to whom they occur. To want to tremble or to be slain in the spirit is a mistake, indeed it can be dangerous. But if they are truly (in some cases at least) manifestations of the Spirit of God that occur during many revivals, then their appearance now may have a much greater significance.

You say, "I don't know. All this makes me fearful. It sounds dangerous." Dangerous? Of course it is dangerous. Who ever heard of a safe war? We are being called to arms. Fear of the enemy can paralyze. This sort of fear is from the enemy and is itself an enemy. Soldiers who are afraid (whether consciously or unconsciously) are at a disadvantage. At best they "beat the air" majoring on talk. At worst they become badly wounded victims in the battle. We are called to fear God and to fear sin (Mt 10:28). We are not called to fear either men or the enemy from whose kingdom we have been delivered, but to march under the banner of a new Master, who plans to put all his enemies beneath his feet.

Part II
Case Studies of the Spirit's Power

Earlier I made the point that power is not without danger. The fact has been reinforced in my mind with the major case studies I engaged in. Of the seven people I spent the most time with I now present only four. I could have presented all seven, but in the interests of honesty I would have had to include the fact that as the manuscript was in its final stages, sin and weakness marred the three stories I have dropped.

In a way I would like to have published them. After all, Scripture includes stories of people who are a mixture of successes and failures. But to protect the privacy of the individuals concerned, I have refrained.

I hold the persons in high esteem. More importantly, I have no doubt either of the genuineness of their relationship with God or of the sacred source of the power in which they walked. Power is never a badge of merit. It is no proof of sanctity, no proof of maturity, no proof of Christian experience or of wisdom. It is seen when a God of grace chooses the weak and foolish to confound the mighty.

Let us all seek to walk in the Spirit's power. But let us never envy those who walk in greater power than we ourselves do, for there are pressures associated with power. Those who walk in power walk also along perilous paths.

11
John Wimber: Pandemonium in the School Gymnasium?

V*ENI, SANCTE SPIRITUS. ET EMITTE COELI- tus Lucis tuae radium.*

Come, Holy Spirit, And from your heavenly seat Send your glorious light.

"Yet that single word which it hears: 'It is I, fear not,' takes all its fear from the soul, and it is most marvellously comforted, and believes that no one will ever be able to make it feel otherwise." THERESA OF AVILA

I said in chapter one that I carried out most (though not all) of my detailed investigations among people affected by John Wimber's ministry. I ought therefore to include a sketch of this controversial man. Many people question the origins of the manifestations in his meetings, declaring they are not of the Spirit. How did he get involved with such phenomena? How did it all start?

When the Pastor Lost Control

John Wimber's introduction to unusual manifestations was unsought, abrupt and unpleasant. It took place on Mothers' Day 1978, in a school gymnasium, the meeting place in those days of the church of which he is still the pastor.

With some misgiving he had permitted a self-invited preacher to conduct the evening service. He was relieved when the young man gave a sound and straightforward address, introducing no heterodox views to the congregation. Wimber found himself settling back to enjoy the service. He was not unduly alarmed even when at the close of his address the young man invited younger members of the congregation who wished to live their lives under the power of the Holy Spirit to come forward. But Wimber's calm was short-lived.

The congregation was predominantly youthful and a large number responded. The speaker waited until they stood before him on the floor of the gymnasium. Older members of the congregation watched, some from chairs on the floor, others from the bleachers. Then he prayed a brief and simple prayer, confessing the Church's failure to give place to the Holy Spirit. He concluded his prayer with the words, "Come, Holy Spirit!"

What followed was electrifying. To Wimber's intense alarm, the young people fell on the floor, some crying out noisily. One young man seemed to be flung forward in such a way that his mouth was jammed over the microphone. Since he was speaking in tongues, his "gibberish" screeched through the public address system. Pandemonium erupted. The young preacher became agitated, shouting excitedly, "More, Lord. More!" At one point, raising his hand he shouted, "Jesus is Lord." The people his hand faced fell untidily around the bleachers.

Wimber was furious. Unable because of the pile of bodies to reach the glossolalia-broadcasting microphone, he called to some young people to remove the young man. They couldn't. The situation was out of control. Wimber's anger increased at the young people's apparent inability to respond to his instructions and at his own inability to regain control of what was happening. Several members of the congregation left in anger, one man slamming his Bible shut before doing so.

Eventually the hubbub in the gymnasium subsided, but the storm in John Wimber's mind had only begun. His peace was destroyed. Once back home he was unable to subdue his agitation. He slept poorly, waking frequently, confused in his thoughts. Anger with the young preacher alternated with worry about his congregation's reaction and bewilderment at the powerful response to the preacher's prayer.

But a deeper doubt haunted his bedroom. It was evident that an extraordinary source of power had invaded the gymnasium. What was its nature? Where had it come from? Was it merely the result of immature judgment on the part of an impulsive young man? The word *pandemonium* (which seemed to describe what had happened) has to do with demons. Was it evil? Could it be of God?

Eventually he gave up on sleep and left the bedroom, going into his study to search the Scriptures. He did not find the prayer, "Come, Holy Spirit!" in the Bible. But he did succeed in finding a number of instances of men trembling and falling under the Spirit's power.

After some time he went out under the stars to pray. As the night wore on he remembered some volumes of church history, and soon was reflecting on events described by Jonathan Edwards, John Wesley and George Whitefield. By now weary in body and mind, but still uncertain and confused, he prayed for clear guidance, and shortly afterward, about 6:30 A.M., received a long-distance telephone call.

The caller was Tom Stipes, a pastor in Denver, who told Wimber he had been awakened early, with the impression that God wanted him to give Wimber a three-word message. Stipes had no idea what

the words might mean.
"What is the message?" Wimber asked, wonderingly.
"It is, 'That was me!' "
That was me. At first he was only aware of shock. Yet as the
words gripped him, they simultaneously released him from his
frustration and fear. Light fell on the events of the previous night
which rearranged themselves reassuringly in his mind. A new certainty grew in him that what had seemed at the time to be horrendous and bizarre had actually come from the dear and familiar hand
of God. With that certainty came peace.

Wimber quickly described to the Denver pastor what had happened, and listened in awe as Stipes, weeping, recounted similar
episodes from his experiences in the early days of the Jesus movement in California.

John Wimber had strong views about the errors of people who
prayed for the sick or who spoke in tongues. He had for most of
his Christian life opposed anything that might represent confusion
or loss of control. But now he was confronted with the fact that
in opposing "supernatural" manifestations he might have been opposing God. C. S. Lewis once commented that he "was dragged
kicking and screaming into the kingdom." This was a similar experience in that I suppose it could be said that Wimber was dragged
kicking and screaming into the era of physical manifestations in the
church he pastored. How had Wimber developed his anticharis-
matic views?

The Making and Breaking of a Rock Musician
John Wimber was born in 1934. His father left the home at the
time of his birth, and his mother reared John for seven years before
her second marriage. He remained an only child.

He describes his upbringing as pagan. *Jesus* was a "cuss word."
At one point, for disciplinary purposes, he was obliged for about
eighteen months to attend a parochial school. But in those days
neither school nor Christianity held any interest for him. He be-

lieves that the limited and distorted view of the faith he picked up there owed more to his lack of interest than to the quality of the instruction. He knew Joseph and Mary had a baby called Jesus and supposed that Jesus was important because of Mary. Some years later when he saw a poster bearing the words "Jesus Saves," he wondered vaguely what it was that Jesus collected.

John's grandfather was led to Christ during his last illness. Immediately before he died he woke from a coma, sat up and, addressing John's mother and grandmother, said, "I've been with Jesus. It's wonderful. It's beautiful. It's glory! It's glory!" He lay down, then sat up again, his arms extended and his face alive with joy, saying, "I'm coming, Jesus." And then he died.[1]

That death in 1952 brought John a strange reassurance about his grandfather. But it did nothing to awaken his curiosity about his grandfather's faith. Nor did it take away dark fears of death that had begun to haunt him shortly before that, and that continued to haunt him for years.

He graduated from high school that same year and from junior college in 1954, having absorbed everything he could about music. Music was to John what the ocean is to a fish. Beginning with a saxophone, a gift from his stepfather, he learned to play several instruments, and for a number of years after leaving college studied composition and orchestration with a private tutor.

Music was soon his bread and butter (and later, his caviar and champagne). Between 1950 and 1962 he gained ninety per cent of his income from teaching, directing, orchestrating and recording music. That latter year found him in Las Vegas, his career soaring and his marriage threatening to fold. He had been busy creating and managing a musical group, The Righteous Brothers, and was also working with a Las Vegas show. His wife, Carol, had left him, taking their children with her, and by October 1962 they had been separated for more than five months. He began to feel desperate.

A friend suggested that he get out into the desert around Las Vegas to seek peace. So one morning he set out to watch the sunrise, hoping to have a religious experience. "I began reflecting on my life," he tells us, "growing more and more despondent. My pregnant wife had left me. My children were gone also. Soon I was weeping." Suddenly, shocked, he heard himself scream, "Oh, God, if you're there, help me!" He wondered if he was going insane.

But back at the hotel a message from Carol awaited him. She wanted to return. Somebody or something had heard his desperate cry, or so it seemed to him. "Well, what d'you know. I'm not crazy. I've made a breakthrough. I'm in touch with the supernatural."

Thinking that the Bible might be a good source of information about God he eventually located a Christian bookstore where he purchased (on the recommendation of the owner of the store, who assured Wimber that it was a real Bible) a paperback copy of a modern translation of the New Testament.

But when in a bar the next day he tried to study his new purchase, a curious waiter asked him what he was doing. John told him. "But that's not a real Bible," the waiter said. "A real Bible has a black cover. On the back it has Holy Bible written on it in gold letters." John had feared as much. The store owner had not given him the real thing! He abandoned the New Testament and hunted until he found a "real" Bible. Then he began to wade through the King James Version of the Pentateuch.

The Wimbers decided to make a determined effort to commit themselves to their marriage. Carol felt it would be better to do so on a religious basis. John had regarded their marriage as essentially civil, for although they had been married by a Baptist pastor, they found him by merely looking up his name in the telephone directory. This time they would be married religiously—in a Catholic church.

Not long after this, one of John's old music friends, Dick, and his wife, Lynn, visited John and Carol to describe their own recent conversion experiences. This in turn led them to attend a Bible study group, led by Gunner Payne, a Quaker who had gone through difficult times (a murdered daughter and prolonged national publicity during the trials) to emerge as a man who lived his life by the values of Christ's kingdom. Payne handled Wimber's voracious but uninformed appetite for Bible knowledge ("I'm not interested in Jesus. I want to find out about God.") with patience and wisdom, molding the enquirer as much by his own character as by all that he knew.

For six weeks John and Carol Wimber continued to attend the Bible studies. But their appetite for knowledge was insatiable. Almost every evening found them at the home of the Paynes, questioning, learning. Then following one of the Bible studies Carol spontaneously declared herself ready to become a Christian and knelt to acknowledge her sin before God. Wimber describes his reaction.

After she finished, the whole group looked over at me. No words were needed to communicate what they were thinking: they expected me to do what Carol had just done. But I decided to hold out. "No way," I thought.

My intransigence was to last no more than thirty seconds. To this day I do not know how or why, but I found myself face down on the floor, weeping. Not praying. Weeping. For half an hour I sobbed. Then I recalled a long-forgotten incident. I remembered a man who used to roam Pershing Square in downtown Los Angeles, wearing sandwich boards. The front board said, "I'm a fool for Christ" and the back said, "Who's fool are you?" I remembered mocking that man—just another religious lunatic walking the streets, I thought at the time.

A strange recollection. Nevertheless Christ spoke powerfully to me through it. He told me that I too must be willing to be a fool for him. Whatever he asked me to do—regardless of the financial, emotional, or physical cost—I was to obey.

I made a sincere but naive decision to be a fool for Christ. . . .[2]

He little knew how much derision and stress he would one day have to face.

The Molding of a Controversial Leader

From that point their lives changed. John's musical career was subsequently abandoned and money given away. Wimber began work at a factory. He also plunged into personal evangelism and began to lead Bible studies. By 1970 he had led many people to faith in Christ and was involved with about five hundred people in different Bible studies. After a while he became the pastor of a Quaker church.

Then from 1970 to 1973, with financial help from friends he attended the Azusa Pacific Bible College, a college with a holiness emphasis. He got more out of the library and from personal conversations with the professors than from the lectures, reading all he could, and acquiring as broad an acquaintance of contemporary Christian movements as could be gleaned from magazines in the library.

His faith in Scripture's authority was never shaken, but his delight in Scripture was undermined by discussions of documentary criticism. But the theological distinctives of the holiness movement left no lasting mark on him. Eventually he came to the firm conclusion that Christian conversion resulted from a work of the Holy Spirit that called for no second work of sanctifying grace, even though the Holy Spirit might thereafter anoint God's servants to meet the exigencies of Christian service.

A year or so after graduating he began to take courses at Fuller Theological Seminary in Pasadena, California, where he was particularly attracted by the teaching of George Eldon Ladd. Later still, intrigued by theories of church growth, he left his own pastoral responsibilities and became the founding director of the Fuller Church Growth Institute. For several years he threw himself energetically into the work of the Institute, traveling the length and breadth of North America, consulted by churches of many denominations on church-growth problems. And in so doing he gained a wide knowledge of the church in the West.

The church-growth movement is associated with the School of

World Missions at Fuller Theological Seminary. Initiated there by the teachings of Dr. Donald McGavran, and carried on by Dr. Peter Wagner, it examines sociological laws that appear to favor the growth of Christian churches. Its exponents in no way wish to undermine the importance of the role of the Holy Spirit, yet to many observers the movement's emphasis on anthropological and sociological principles is suspect. Critics view church-growth proponents as being too pragmatic, as believing that whatever works must therefore also be good and true, placing more faith in their grasp of functional principles than in the power of God.

It would be interesting to know whether Wimber was at heart a pragmatist during those years. Certainly he is not one now. While he retains a strong interest in the dynamics of church growth, he is too awed by the sovereign acts of God, too concerned about the reconciling thrust of the gospel to make a pragmatist.

Yet for a variety of reasons Wimber largely lost his Christian joy during his time with the Church Growth Institute. His conscience was a little bothered by the fees he collected from churches who consulted him. He had become self-indulgent and was dangerously overweight. He grew dissatisfied, even cynical, and experienced progressively failing health. Eventually he left the Church Growth Institute. He accepted responsibility for a Bible study group his wife had started in their home.

A firm opponent of tongues and healing, Carol Wimber had preached against them to women's groups all over the county where they lived. She had also been instrumental in having several people who believed in such things removed from the church.

One night she dreamed she was giving her usual seven-point message against tongues, only to wake after the sixth point to find herself doing exactly what she had so often preached against—speaking in tongues. Over the next three weeks she wept frequently, repenting bitterly of her past attitude and going out of her way to apologize to those whom she had wronged in her attacks about the issue.

Carol Wimber then began to attend the Twin Peaks Calvary Chapel. (The Calvary Chapels arose from evangelism among the Jesus people, a work carried out by Chuck Smith, originally a member of a Four Square church.) Occasionally her husband would accompany her. So when eventually the Wimber's home study group decided to become a church, Don McClure, the pastor of Twin Peaks, suggested the new church be affiliated with his. Wimber asked about the conditions of such an attachment, and receiving an assurance of their doctrinal autonomy (to this day Wimber remains committed to the theological views expressed in the Westminster Confession, and in particular to its view of sanctification) the smaller group accepted the offer.

It was an arrangement doomed not to work. The catastrophic events of that fateful Mothers' Day when so many young people had fallen on the floor created concern in the Calvary Chapels, and it was suggested that the Wimbers' group, now very much larger than at its inception, disassociate from the Calvary Chapels and affiliate with the Vineyard movement, a tiny group of churches that had previously separated from the Calvary Chapels.

It was the beginning of an association that has continued to this day and that has led to the enormous growth of the Vineyard movement, a movement of which John Wimber is the unofficial leader.[3]

A Personality Profile

What of the man himself? How does he strike observers who talk to him privately? His good friend David Watson described him as "a large, lovable, warm and gentle person, reminding me of a favorite teddy bear. He also has an able mind, wide Christian experience and shrewd spiritual discernment."[4] My impression is also of a warm and gentle man, perhaps a little shy, yet a man who knows where he is going, and who stubbornly drives himself (and sometimes others) to get there. Like most leaders he likes his own way and can at times be demanding, yet his personal integrity is matched both by his compassion, his respect for others, and by his drive to proclaim. Most people who meet him personally like him. Watson's view is also correct that he is widely read and an astute thinker. He has the kind of humility that is ready to acknowledge his areas of weakness, both intellectual and personal, and is diligent in correcting them. He welcomes new information and counsel. If anything, he shows too much respect for other people's areas of expertise. Some criticism he receives is cruel and unjust, but in whatever spirit it is given and however much he may be wounded by it, he considers it carefully before deciding whether to accept or reject it. While he may make strongly critical statements about the church as a whole, his emphasis is on our common failures in the church rather than hatred of those who abuse him.

His attitude to the church at large became clear in a message he gave recently to the Vineyard Christian Fellowship in Anaheim. "We do not have any new doctrine to bring to the Church. . . . It would be nice (but a little naive) for us to believe that we had arrived at the fullness of the faith. . . . We are not the whole of the Church, we are just a small part of the Church Universal. . . . We affirm in general all the historic creeds . . . and I affirm the historic churches. God raised them up. . . ."

Among the various credal statements, the one that means the most to him, partly because of its comprehensive nature, is the Westminster Confession. From his early association (following his conversion) with Quaker churches, he has in addition retained a concern "for the poor, the broken—and what we must do for them. . . ." but while deploring war and violence, Wimber quietly rejects the pacifism of the Friends. Typical of his approach to Christianity is his repeated assertion that "neither experience, nor gifts, nor even doctrinal correctness are of value unless they contribute to holy living."

Let me focus now on Wimber as a man whose preaching is associated with the religious experiences we are studying. How do we account for the things that happened to him? Neither John nor

Carol Wimber are people who change their attitudes easily. What happened to both of them has something in common to what happened to Paul on the Damascus road. I am not saying that all their opinions are correct because they had dramatic experiences. Truth comes from Scripture. Rather I am saying two things. First, it interests me that God not infrequently chooses for a servant someone who stubbornly opposes him. Second, I am also more inclined to attach weight to a stubborn opinion which has taken a one-hundred-eighty-degree turn.

This chapter began with an account of a man who was furious when manifestations broke out in his own church. My guess would be that he resented not being in control. Certainly he was also alarmed at the potential loss of support. He wanted nothing to do with outbreaks of that sort.

I would venture to suggest that this (clinging to control) represented sin on Wimber's part. From his own conversion experience he knew what it was to lose control. As his wife had made her confession of Christ, Wimber had firmly decided that he was not going to accede to group expectations.

But when he joined his wife on the floor, he began weeping uncontrollably in an obvious manifestation of the Spirit's power. In the presence of onlookers he was forcefully humbled "face down" before his Savior. And in deep repentance he had decided to be willing to be a fool for Christ's sake. The incident in the school gymnasium was Christ's reminder of the covenant between them.

It is in that sense his experience parallels that of the apostle Paul. First, there was the humiliation of the manner of his conversion. Then as a successful pastor of a growing church he had been forced to recognize the hand of God (against his own preferences and better judgment) in the events that had occurred in the gymnasium. If he had been an enthusiastic supporter of revivals and the manifestations that accompany them, their appearance in his ministry would have been suspect. The fact is that he had hated and feared them until he was forced to acknowledge the hand of God.

But you may ask: Could not the confusion in the service plus the telephone call from Denver have reflected Satanic deception? Hardly. Satan begins by seducing and alluring. He winds up by destroying. He does not begin by making somebody look foolish. For Wimber the incident was a humiliation. He lost control of the service and he lost church members. He had to learn again that the church was not his church but God's church, and that God conducts affairs as he pleases. He also was forcefully reminded of God's word to him at his conversion—that he would have to be willing to look like a fool.

Indeed the experiences that have followed have included their share of mockery, stresses and humiliations for John Wimber. He has felt them keenly and at times they have wounded him deeply, even though he might retain an outward calm and comment wryly, "They come with the job."

But as I pointed out in chapter three, revivals shake the foundations of the very institutions that arose from previous revivals. Old leaders resent new upstarts, especially (as is frequently the case) when the upstarts are not from the oldest denominations or the finest academic institutions, or are not at least card-carrying Ph.D.'s.

We are therefore dismayed by the Wimbers and the Annacondias of this world, the preacher upstarts. We hasten to point out that "such people" have sometimes done a lot of harm. Preachers are a touchy bunch. (If you stand out you get flak—until you make the big time, at which point you are awarded an honorary doctorate.) This is not as it should be. The real test of whether we are "determined to know nothing save Jesus Christ and him crucified" comes when we encounter someone with less formal training who is more greatly used than we are. Lloyd-Jones does well to comment:

> If your doctrine of the Holy Spirit does not include this idea of
> the Holy Spirit falling on people, it is seriously, grievously de-

fective. This, it seems to me, has been the trouble especially during this present century, indeed almost for a hundred years. The whole notion of the Holy Spirit falling on people has been discountenanced and discouraged, and if you read many of the books on the Holy Spirit you will find it is not even mentioned at all, a fact which is surely one of the prime explanations of the present state of the Christian church. . . . Suddenly we all became so respectable and so learned and people said, "Ah, that old type of preaching is no longer good enough, the people are now receiving education". . . . Then followed that most devastating thing that has affected the life of the church—Victorianism. It entered into the churches, particularly the Free Churches . . . and the great word became "dignity." Dignity! Formality! Learning! Culture![5]

But let me get back to the fear that I have discussed several times, the fear of demonic deception. For many people Carol Wimber's conversion to tongues raises the matter once again. Let me say at once that if her dream, along with the awakening to find herself speaking in tongues was of the devil, then we are all in a sorry plight. If the devil can come along at any time and so overwhelm a Christian's ardent opposition to tongues (or anything else) in such a manner, then heaven help us all!

The point at issue is not the validity of tongues but the possibility of deception. Carol Wimber's experience echoes the experience of Peter having a vision of the "unclean" animals and being told to eat them, or, again of Paul's being overcome on the Damascus road. In both cases opposition to God is powerfully and humiliatingly stopped. Satan cannot do that. Only God can. Satan's deception (as in Eden) is always low-key. And it never results in repentance for sin.

Peter and Paul both repented—not of their wrong doctrine but of their sin. In Carol Wimber's case it was a repentance that led to apologies to persons she had wounded. Does Satan delight in repentance, confession of sinful attitudes and reconciliation among believers? Of course not! Only the Spirit heals broken relationships.

How then is it that I have insisted all along that revivals are accompanied by divisions among God's people? How is it that the outbreak of manifestations in Wimber's church led to a parting of the ways with Chuck Smith? Was the Spirit behind that?

Of course not. In chapter three we looked at the reasons. God does not approve of them. Divisions commonly arise because of carnality among Christians. And revived Christians share in the carnality at times. And when they arise each side blames the other for the division. The enemy of our souls who hates revival fans the fires of our jealousies and our resentments. In the case of John and Carol Wimber, however, I am impressed by the restraint and the charity with which, even in private, they speak of their critics.

While we should not encourage bitter criticism, certainly no Christian leader or movement is above careful evaluation. So in the next chapter we will take a closer look at the strengths and weakness of both.

12
John Wimber and the Vineyard Movement

O F ALL THE CANTS THAT ARE CANTED IN *this canting world—though the cant of hypocrites may be the worst—the cant of criticism is the most tormenting."* LAURENCE STERNE

As I travel, I am often asked, "What do you think of John Wimber and the Vineyard movement?" I must have made it clear already in this book that I admire and respect John Wimber, seeing him as a man of integrity, of warmth, humility and courage. Being human he is imperfect and makes no pretense of being otherwise. He knows he has limitations, and he knows he has made mistakes. But he has the faith and the guts to seek to do the will of God as he understands it, and God seems to be with him in the things he does.

Even though Matthew Arnold was primarily speaking of literary criticism, I still like the way he defined criticism, ". . . a disinterested endeavour to learn and propagate the best that is known and thought . . ." By disinterested he meant unbiased, nonpartisan. It is certainly my desire to be nonpartisan, to not exalt one Christian movement over another but to see God's people one in spirit, bound together harmoniously in Christ.

Wimber has been subjected to a great deal of criticism, much of it unjust and ill-informed. Being human he has been wounded by it, yet remains remarkably restrained, not replying in kind. Because of this reason I hesitate to add to his burdens. But throughout this book I have been looking at revival as having two sides—a human and a divine. The divine side we can only accept with gratitude and awe. The human side will always be fallible.

My studies for this book focused on behavioral manifestations and on the people who experienced them, not on the movement as a whole. I have visited only a small number of Vineyard churches and attended a dozen or more Vineyard conferences, enough to give me somewhat of an idea about what is going on, but hardly enough to do a global evaluation. Thus an evaluation of the movement has been secondary for me.

The principal question in my mind when I have been present at some of the conferences and meetings has been, "Is this revival?" Let me hark back to the criteria of an earlier chapter. In it I tried to extract the most significant elements in the Great Awakening. Let us review these:

First, *converted and unconverted men, women and children, stunned by a vision both of God's holiness and his mercy, are awakened in large numbers to repentance, faith and worship.* At Vineyard conferences I have seen this. Healings may have made people more willing to listen, but preaching that brought a sense of God's holiness was what wrought the change. At the Vineyard Church of Anaheim and in other areas I have seen evidence that the results are ongoing.

Second, *God's power is manifest in human lives in ways no psycho-*

logical or sociological laws can explain adequately. In those meetings I have attended, this has also been the case.

Third, *the community as a whole becomes aware of what is happening, many perceiving the movement as a threat to existing institutions.* When in an earlier chapter I used the expression "the whole community," I meant the wider community of town, city or country. Certainly religious communities and institutions have become aware of what is happening through Vineyard, and many of these have indeed perceived the movement as a threat to existing institutions. As yet I am not aware that the wider nonreligious community has reacted in this way.

Fourth, *some men and women exhibit unusual physical and emotional manifestations. These create controversy. They can be an offense to opponents of the revival and a snare to its supporters.* This has been the case with the Vineyard movement as indicated already.

Fifth, *some revived Christians behave in an immature and impulsive way, while others fall into sin. In this way the revival appears to be a strange blend of godly and ungodly influences, of displays of divine power and of human weakness.* As in past movements of the Spirit, some of the men and women influenced by the Holy Spirit through the Vineyard movement have behaved in immature and foolish ways. Some have fallen into sin. The Holy Spirit has clearly not been doling out sinless perfection. But I observe that the behavior has produced a reaction within the movement to correct and to learn from experience.

Sixth, *wherever the revival is extensive enough to have national impact, sociopolitical reform follows over the succeeding century. In this way Christ's kingdom begins to be exercised over the evils of oppression and injustice.* In my judgment the current revival is, as I write this book, a long way from being extensive enough to have a major impact on national life. It would be foolish to pretend otherwise. But I believe God is in it.

The seeds of such reform are certainly present. Eddie Gibbs of Fuller Theological Seminary in Pasadena reports: "There is no undue emphasis on supernatural phenomena; the teaching is on a broadly based Biblical diet of faithful expository preaching. And the church stimulates an impressive range of social-concern ministries, including prison visitation, caring for the homes and needs of the elderly, and ministry among the poor in Mexico."[1] I hope and pray that such activities may go as far and farther than the Great Awakening of the eighteenth century.

Earlier I compared revival with forest fires. We must keep in mind that we are dealing not just with the Third Wave in the West (Pentecostalism of the early 1900s being the first wave and the Charismatic renewal of more recent decades being the second), but with revival movements in cities and countries on every major continent. Some revivals are fairly localized and brief. Occasionally smaller revival fires coalesce, so that something comparable with the Great Awakening results. The Vineyard movement is not at this point comparable with the Great Awakening. But in the sense that the Holy Spirit manifests his power through the movement, not only in behavioral manifestations and the healing of the sick, but bringing Christians to repentance, more holiness and more power for service, and in awakening numbers of the unconverted, it most certainly does represent revival in its early stages.

It is our duty to pray to God the Father that the Holy Spirit will continue to work through what some have called the Third Wave, and through what other agencies he may choose, to bring a second and greater awakening to pass.

Prophet and Builder

To talk about the Vineyard movement is to talk about two things. One is a small but rapidly growing affiliation of churches that goes by that name. Another, more importantly, is the impact that John Wimber's demonstration of signs and wonders is having on other churches and denominations, some of whose traditions are far removed from reformed Christianity. The movement is also extending into the Roman Catholic Church.

In fact Wimber's deepest interests do not appear to lie in founding a denomination. He longs to spread the message of the Third Wave among the church at large, the church worldwide. He is, therefore, a man torn in several directions. He struggles to be pastorally responsible to the Anaheim Vineyard in southern California, to be pastorally and administratively responsible to the growing Vineyard denomination, and to deliver a message to the church worldwide. In attempting to do all three he does none of them as well as he could if he were not stuck with the others. He may well be killing himself in the process.

Is Wimber being irresponsible in attempting so much when many people are looking to him for a degree of leadership he cannot possibly provide? I have thought long about the question. In a sense he is like the boy who put his finger in the dike, not fully realizing the pressures that would follow. I do not believe that he is irresponsible, but I believe he will be if he goes on as he has in the past.

One mistake is fundamental. You cannot be simultaneously a builder (at least a good builder) and a prophet. It may be possible to be both at the inception of a movement, but to the degree the movement grows, the difficulty increases.

During the Great Awakening Whitefield wound up as the "prophet" and Wesley the builder. Their roles were at first indistinguishable, but Whitefield at one point in his life deliberately chose to contribute to the church at large. At that point he concerned himself less with the "societies." For this reason no denomination commemorates his name and work. Wesley, on the other hand, never ceased to be a builder, and built carefully on the class and society structure, which later became first one and later several denominations. It is universally recognized that his careful organizational structuring of the future denomination was crucial to the revival movement. I believe Whitefield made an even greater contribution to the Great Awakening than Wesley. But both of their roles were essential to its abiding power.

Both Wesley and Whitefield possessed the gifts to fill either role. Whitefield's early work in founding societies, as well as his missionary work in Georgia, demonstrated that. Wesley had tremendous evangelistic and preaching gifts, not as great as Whitefield's perhaps, but still extraordinary.

The crucial question does not have to do with giftedness, but with the heart. Whatever gifts one has, there is room in one's heart only for the task and the burden the Holy Spirit lays on it. Whitefield and Wesley, despite the uneasiness of their on-off relationship, wound up doing what their real burden was given for. My prayer for Wimber is that he will discern what that is and release the rest.

Vineyard Churches

New and rapidly growing movements invariably have problems. If you jam up a river you get problems when the log jam breaks. And revivals and reformations represent the breaking of a jam—or even of a dam.

The damage of a bursting log jam shows up in several ways. First, new movements attract not only higher proportions of less educated groups, but also of the unstable and the dissatisfied. Second, where the new emphasis is concerned, the led (including the untrained and the disgruntled led) are often more extreme than the original leaders. Third, appointment of leaders made early in the movement history will include a number of unwise choices. Insecurity in younger leaders tends to make some of them arrogant and rigid. Fourth, the real leaders are powerfully impressive. Many younger leaders in modeling themselves on them can become stereotyped in their manner and present a caricature of the message.

These factors combine to push the early movement into an exaggerated emphasis on its special contribution. This contribution may need to be proclaimed. Sadly, it is often the caricature (presented by immature leaders and the less sophisticated followers) that gets across to the church at large, increasing the resistance to whatever is good and needed from the movement.

It would be unwise to attempt at this early stage a definitive evaluation of the nascent denomination called Vineyard. Most of its features are encouraging. Certainly if one views it as a whole it is alive, effective evangelistically, fervent in worship and, in my view, sound in doctrine. But dangerous shoals lie ahead of it. The rapidity of its growth exposes it to the many hazards associated with newness and explosive development. I wish that there could be more consistent senior input into local churches. But only the future will tell what will happen to the movement. Most significant movements start by being a little wild, settle down to a respectable middle age, then, rejoicing in their respectability, relax into a creeping death. Still, I am not pessimistic.

The association of Vineyard churches grows in three ways. Teams from larger churches establish new churches, often in areas where they have engaged in evangelism. New churches may also spring up in areas where seminars are held. These are commonly sponsored by independent groups of local Christians. Third, churches already in existence may apply for association with the movement, many of them churches that are disenchanted with their parent denomination. (At one point in 1986, over a hundred of these churches had already applied for association with the movement, and understandably they varied enormously in their motivation, leadership and maturity. Some churches were eventually accepted, others not.) The three kinds of church make up the movement in roughly equal proportions.

Power evangelism, one of Wimber's more controversial emphases, is the idea that signs of God's power open the hearts of unconverted to the gospel. Critics who deplore power evangelism point out that the spectacular tends to take the spotlight away from the need for personal holiness and a disciplined walk. This is true, and perhaps inevitable—at least in the initial stages of the movement.

During the past hundred years we have seen how powerful

healers have fallen prey to the temptations power exposes them to. Greed, lust, dishonesty, arrogance, along with their demonic minions move like an army of saboteurs and fifth columnists into any church or movement gifted with power. It happened in Corinth, and Paul saw it clearly. And through his servant John, the Lord of the Church rebuked similar trends in the church in Thyatira (Rev 2:18-22). I take it as axiomatic that wherever Satan sees power, he sows sin. We are fools if we forget this.

So far as John Wimber is concerned, holiness is a major personal preoccupation and a constant theme of his domestic preaching. But success attracts unstable Christians as well as mature ones. As I talk to rank-and-file members of the movement, as well as with a few of the pastors, I find a mixture of those whose hearts are on fire for God and a smaller number who are less mature and whose conversation tends to focus on healings and words of knowledge more than with the battle with personal sin. One pastor, in a discussion on pseudoreligiosity, even said with unfortunate humor, "You know, a little sin stops us from being too religious!"

Signs and wonders are often present when sin is defeated. Men and women are dramatically delivered as the chains of sexual sin and drug addiction are broken in prayer. People who have such experiences often know and feel the deliverance as it takes place. Little wonder that the Devil should sow sin where power is manifest!

But deliverance from the chains of sin is normally a less dramatic affair in which subjective experiences play only a small part. The ongoing process of sanctification is a battle to believe and receive what God has revealed in his Word. Since many of us are by nature predisposed to enjoy spectacular solutions to problems it is of the utmost importance that additional emphasis be placed on who we are in Christ and in the objective nature of his triumphs.

In the Anaheim Vineyard, Carol Wimber and Gloria Thomson stress the objective nature of Christ's saving work, of the Christian's position in Christ and participation in the fruits of that work.

In regular classes they warn against the very danger I am speaking of. Again, the latest catalog of Vineyard tapes and teaching materials reveals that a corrective trend is well established. Just over half the tapes are devoted to topics such as Christian discipleship and growth and issues such as repentance.

Power Evangelism

If the assertions underlying power evangelism are true (as I believe they are), it would be a mistake to soft-pedal the movement's message to the church around the globe simply because immature Christians focus on it to the exclusion of more important things. But is it true that signs and wonders awaken interest in the gospel? Critics of the movement focus on the word *normative*. In effect they say that yes, miracles can happen, but Wimber is wrong to accuse Wesley, Whitefield, Moody and Billy Sunday of subnormal evangelism. Actually Wimber doesn't do any such thing, but his critics see him doing so by implication.

The Oxford English Dictionary defines normative as "establishing or setting up a norm or standard." Wimber's main point is that evangelism takes place more easily wherever signs and wonders occur. That is an indisputably biblical point. What I also see as biblical is his assertion that healings and the casting out of demons can be expected to occur if we move in the authority of the kingdom. They do not always occur, but they should be looked for. Not everyone agrees that the view is biblical, but since I have observed not only accelerated healings, but something of the miraculous in Vineyard conferences, I would say that Wimber's view of what Scripture says has powerful backing.

The suggestion that in making the point he is downgrading the evangelism of Wesley, Whitefield, Moody and Graham is rather silly. In the first place Wimber is the first to acknowledge that regeneration is the greatest miracle of all. The astonishing number of conversions in Moody's meetings is itself a miracle. And undoubtedly the evidence of changed lives has done much during the past three hundred years to awaken the interest of skeptics and hardened sinners.

I would define power evangelism as that sort of evangelism where the unsaved are compelled to pay attention by unmistakable evidence that a God of supernatural power is present. The "signs and wonders" may be the kinds of things I have been discussing in this book. Commonly in Jesus' day they were healings, including the healing of demoniacs. On the day of Pentecost it was the public spectacle of ignorant men speaking in known languages. At certain points in history it has been the stunning nature of radical conversions en masse.

As I have pointed out elsewhere, one can hardly accuse Wesley of not making use of signs and wonders. For him, the outcries, the tremblings, the fallings on the ground were supernatural, were signs and wonders that awakened a response. As mentioned in chapter nine, John Cennick reported of Wesley, "Frequently when none were agitated in the meetings, he prayed, Lord! where are thy tokens and signs, and I don't remember ever to have seen it otherwise than that on his so praying several were seized."[2]

Whitefield consistently saw the more subdued weeping and a certain amount of falling or "being overcome." More importantly, both Wesley and Whitefield were empowered by a special anointing of the Holy Spirit in their evangelism. It was this that preceded and empowered their evangelism. Wesley describes the occasion in his journal.

Mon. Jan. 1, 1739.—Mr. Hall, Kinchin, Ingham, Whitefield, Hutchins and my brother Charles, were present at our love-feast in Fetter Lane, with about sixty of our brethren. About three in the morning, as we were continuing instant in prayer, the power of God came mightily upon us, insomuch than many cried out for exceeding joy, and many fell to the ground. As soon as we were recovered a little from that awe and amazement at the presence of his Majesty, we broke out with one voice, "We praise thee, O God; we acknowledge thee to be the Lord."[3]

The "supernatural" elements in their ministries became more obvious after this. The point at issue is not the particular manifestation of power, whether it should be Wesley's and Whitefield's signs or Wimber's, whether it should be crying out, mass conversions, mass weeping or falling, or whether healings should also take place. Wesley, and Whitefield had been anointed with power from on high. Each operated in the power arising from that anointing, and the nature of their work reflects this.

And Moody? As mentioned in chapter two, Moody's evangelism was radically changed following the day when in New York he had an extraordinary experience of God's love. "The sermons were not different; I did not present any new truths, and yet hundreds were converted."[4] It was immediately following this experience during his second and more extended mission in Britain, that the results of his own preaching bewildered him. Following his second meeting,

he asked all who would like to become Christians to rise, that he might pray for them. People rose all over the house until it seemed as if the whole audience was getting up.

Mr. Moody said to himself, "These people don't understand me. They don't know what I mean when I ask them to rise." He had never seen such results before, and did not know what to make of it. . . . The minister was surprised, and so was Mr. Moody. Neither had expected such a blessing. . . . When Mr. Moody again asked those that really wanted to become Christians to rise, the whole audience got up.[5]

In contrast, much contemporary evangelism appears to depend more on human persuasiveness than on divine power. What the Spirit did through Moody has become a method, a technique.

Church Growth

The topic of church growth is de rigueur in many circles, and it is also a prominent element in the Third Wave. Personally I deplore the pragmatic approach that many church-growth advocates adopt.

Christianity may be practical, but it is never pragmatic. Christianity is water and pragmatism is oil.

In the previous chapter I made Wimber's nonpragmatic attitude to church growth clear. His watch cry would be, "Suffer the churches to grow, and forbid them not," rather than, "Let us employ those laws by which we can make churches grow." But despite this the message that seems to reach many pastors is, "The best churches are big churches." (Interestingly, and with certain exceptions, they also grow best in California.) Perhaps the message comes across because Wimber team-teaches church growth along with his friend Peter Wagner.

I have come across a number of Vineyard pastors, and one or two pastors of other denominations affected by the movement, who are convinced that bigness is good and that large churches are a good thing. They certainly can be in that they have human, spiritual and financial resources smaller churches lack. It is also true that many small churches fail to grow because they are making stupid mistakes rather than because they lack faithfulness. At this point church-growth principles can be helpful. But we must not forget that there are special advantages that small churches have—especially when persecution starts and the church has to go underground.

Risk-taking and Obedience

People who find themselves part of the excitement of a new wave, whether they are leaders or led, find taking risks a little easier. The Vineyard movement encourages such risks as the establishing of new churches. I see this as a refreshing change in a Christendom where caution and prudence are often a substitute for faith, and a reflection of belief in a small God.

The Vineyard philosophy is actually one of pointing out that obedience to God commonly involves risk. Even in the issue of divine healing, the teaching can be summarized: Prayer for healing is a matter of obedience and must reflect compassion for the sufferer. We do not wait for a special sign to heal but run the risk of looking like a fool. Needless to say, everything hinges on knowing the will of God.

The movement does not teach risk-taking for its own sake. But there are always people who take risks for the wrong reasons, often to compensate for an unconscious fear of cowardice. I have known would-be church planters ignore advice to stick around longer with a parent church before embarking on the great venture. The pain of what followed was real. Some church planters have emerged from the ordeal wiser and more mature. Others remain wounded and ineffective. I believe local Vineyard leaders must get tougher with the problem. For their own sake and for the church's, disciplinary action must be taken against those who proceed without the blessing of parent churches.

Again, parent churches can be too ambitious in establishing daughter churches, especially where the church planting involves an exodus of church members to the daughter church. The Anaheim Vineyard planted four new churches over a period of a year or so, and lost many hundreds of members in the process. The churches are doing well, but the parent church suffered a severe depletion of middle leadership.

The Vineyard and Prophecy

Christians differ as to whether prophetic gifts survive in today's church. Those who oppose the idea fear false prophecy, and obviously false prophecy has always been and will always be a danger to God's people. One particular fear is that prophecy may be conceived of as that kind of revelation that adds to Scripture. Vineyard is clear on the issue. Prophecy may predict future events, but its purpose is to admonish, instruct and encourage God's people. Prophetic utterances must always be subservient to Scripture and under the authority of the church's leaders.

Wimber's attitude to prophetic gifts is reflected throughout the movement. He would rather encourage and train men and women who show prophetic gifting than to squelch prophecy within the church. Most "prophecies" I have heard in Vineyard churches have been bland utterances which could be summed up in the words, "God loves you, folks." They are hardly dangerous, and may not have anything to do with the prophetic utterances found in Scripture.

But not all are so. Sometimes I got the feeling that there was a mixture of a message from God and the emotions and insecurities of the person speaking. It was almost as though the person was partly editing and partly developing a script. On other occasions something of unique power and brevity came across.

My own extremely limited experience of this sort of thing has been of something which came wordlessly, as a totality and in a split second, with such clarity, force and insistence that I had to write the wordless "thing" in words, trembling all the time lest I misinterpret by the slightest nuance what was communicated. But I can only speak for myself. I am reminded of Underhill's description, "Their character [of certain communications from God] is less that of messages than of 'invasions' from beyond the threshold; transcending succession and conveying 'all at once' . . . truth or certitude."[6]

The most common prophetic manifestation is of what are called words of knowledge. Whether these are words of knowledge as understood by the Corinthian church is hard to say. What I have observed is a prophetic manifestation of impressive accuracy and sometimes of impressive detail, describing either physical conditions or the emotional disturbances and thoughts of individual people present that could not possibly have been known to the person who had the word of knowledge.

I have more concern about these than about prophecy in general, and my concern arises precisely because of the power and the effectiveness of the genuine article. I am astonished at the rapidity with which Christians can learn and develop the gift. It naturally follows that anyone who has seen this will want to enable the church at large to acquire it, and large seminars would seem an ideal opportunity.

But I am not sure whether the advantages of teaching the use of words of knowledge publicly, are not outweighed by the risks and disadvantages of doing so. The public teaching seems to me too uncontrolled and inadequately safeguarded. I have seen enough of phony words of knowledge to realize that some people return to their churches and groups where with inadequate counsel and supervision they display their own productions.

The Vineyard and Worship

Worship is extremely important in the movement. Most Vineyard services begin with thirty to forty minutes of worship. The worship is expressed in simple songs in a musical idiom somewhere between soft rock and "easy listening." The music appeals widely to the beat generation, and the simplicity of the lyrics is comprehensible to the unchurched and often refreshing to people with quite a sophisticated religious background. I believe the latter react to the empty formalism which has stripped great hymns of their true worth in many churches. Vineyard songs also reenact history in the sense that all religious movements initially produce a hymnology in a contemporary lyrical and musical tradition.

What I find refreshing is that people *worship* at Vineyard conferences. The worship leader, usually backed by a small group of instrumentalists, is not leading singing, but worship. Tempo may be determined by the musical group, but that is incidental. The group conceives its own function as one of worshiping.

The powerful effect that the worship has is sometimes explained as being due to a hypnotic effect of the singing of a song several times. As a psychiatrist with a good deal of (I regret to say) experience and observation of hypnosis, I find the idea absurd. There are other reasons for repetition than hypnosis. Cherubim are very repetitious in their worship. "Day and night they never stop saying, 'Holy, holy, holy is the Lord God Almighty, who was, and is, and is to come' " (Rev 4:8). Sometimes repetition is the only way one can relieve oneself of the yearning to express that which is too deep to express easily.

People are free to stand, kneel or sit as they worship, and many raise their hands from time to time in "charismatic" fashion. Some Christians see such expressions as virtuous, others as reprehensible. To me they are merely cultural, and in themselves neither good nor bad. What matters is what they are expressions of. If they are merely an expression of conforming to what everyone else is doing, they are valueless. Where they are genuine expressions of adoration and gratitude they are a sweet smell in God's nostrils. All Christians, charismatics included, must be more tolerant about cultural expressions of worship, and look at worship from God's perspective.

My personal reaction in Vineyard services is mixed. On the one hand I generally warm to the genuineness of what is going on. On the other I have some trouble both with the musical idiom, with the cultural expression of worship and with what ultimately will prove to be a shallowness in the concepts in some of the lyrics.

The musical idiom is the least important of these. Some of the music is extremely good and even though it is not my favorite I have learned to appreciate it. My own background is formal. Raising my arms is often difficult—and my difficulty has nothing to do with freedom in the Spirit. In the solitude of my chamber I have for many years stood, walked, sat, stamped my feet, lain on the floor, laughed, cried, sung, shouted, talked or remained silent. But in public it is still hard for me to shed my Britishness. However, I am trying, and am learning little by little to "do my own thing" when I attend a Vineyard service and even when I attend more formal kinds of church service.

I believe worship involves the whole person, body, soul and spirit. It involves the body not only in the sense that I express worship in my culturally learned body language (often without realizing I do so) but in the sense that I should perform every single task in life as an act of worship. I should even clean my teeth for the glory of my Redeemer.

Worship involves my will. I choose to worship. Yet ideally it also involves my emotions, and may become fervent and passionate in the degree that it does so. At its highest it is both objective (the glories of God are real, and rightly compel my adoration) and subjective. God's glory is meant also to be subjectively appreciated and entered into. Worship involves my intellect and my spirit, in that both are necessary if I am in any sense to comprehend the incomprehensible.

But to define depth of worship in terms of conceptualization is difficult. Let me put it this way. While it is our duty to worship whether we feel like doing so or not, worship flows best when our hearts burn with passion. Mine burns when the Spirit reveals God's glories to me anew. The revelations, and to some extent the expressions, have come from Scripture. They have also come from an acquaintance with the worship forms and the liturgies of the church down the ages. I find as I meditate on a psalm, on a fourth-century hymn, on the old Anglican communion service in the Book of Common Prayer or on the private devotions of Lancelot Andrewes, that my spirit is able to expand its horizons, and that worship grows in depth as well as passion.

Vineyard worship is great—for now. It won't be great thirty years down the line unless it grows by benefiting from past ages. Wimber realizes this, and tries to introduce older hymns.

A Future of Problems and Promise

The Vineyard movement has begun as have many Christian movements, great and small, throughout history. Its origins, I believe, were of God. Its development has been a fallible human response to what the Holy Spirit is seeking to do in and to our generation.

Christians react to it as they have always reacted to a new movement, some with naive enthusiasm, others with sober caution, still others with fear, suspicion and hostility. Many people have been won for Christ and many more have been spiritually quickened and some have been attracted to the movement from their own churches or denominations. Some pastors have found a new lease on life and a profound new purpose in life, though others have changed horses in midstream for inadequate reasons.

The movement's emphases and worship style have much to teach us. They are needed. But by the same token the movement must beware of getting them out of proportion. Wimber's clear understanding that practical holiness must be emphasized more and more is to be welcomed.

I believe the real reason for the impact is that the Holy Spirit is opening the eyes of Christians to the need for and the possibilities of Christ's authority and power. The Spirit seems to use different methods in different ages. If he chooses to manifest his evangelistic power through healing, we must be cautious about despising what he does. The message of the Third Wave is an important one. It is true and it is needed in today's church.

Many of the movement's problems spring from the rapidity of its growth and the worldwide scope of its operations in Europe, Asia, South Africa, North America and the Antipodes. Immature enthusiasm on the part of converts to a movement (who may neglect personal holiness because of more exciting stuff) is an inevitable problem and one that can be corrected. In addition, Vineyard pastors often face a lonely struggle with what they perceive as inadequate back-up from the Vineyard movement. If the present rate of expansion continues they are unlikely to get the degree of support they desire very soon. Some will thrive, others may wither or burn out. But power evangelism must not be eliminated because of the problems.

There is great promise in the movement. Its most important feature is the impact it is having on other churches and denominations. As Tim Stafford writes, the movement "carries a surge of evangelism, of praise, of expectation of the Spirit's power. It reopens forgotten modes of ministry. John Wimber challenges the evangelical church not to live by its techniques and its programs, but by the Spirit—not to harden its expectations of the way God ought to act, but to become open to the surprising works of God."[7] In this way the Vineyard could be a further factor in fomenting worldwide revival. Whether it will so prove remains to be seen.

13

Sandy: The Voice on the Stereo

A HAND TOUCHED ME AND SET ME TREM-
bling on my hands and knees." DANIEL THE PROPHET

One morning during a Vineyard conference in 1984, Sandy Solomon was prayed for by John and Carol Wimber. As they prayed,
Sandy felt "tremendous energy" coursing through her body. She
fell and became aware that her hands and feet were "hitting the
floor" rhythmically. "I couldn't stop it. . . ." She was unaware of
the passage of time and eventually the extreme shaking subsided.
She heard John Wimber asking her how she was and telling her,
as he helped her to her feet, that the Holy Spirit still seemed to be
resting on her. She estimated she had been on the floor for ten to
fifteen minutes and was surprised to find that she had been "out"

for about an hour and a half.

Wimber asked her to pray for someone else. As she raised her hands to do so "the Spirit came on me again." She fell and heard Wimber say, "There she goes again!" This time she thought she was affected about five to ten minutes, but in fact was on the floor for an hour and a half. She has had several such experiences on subsequent occasions.

I mention Sandy's story for several reasons. It reminds us that manifestations (whether they be falling, trembling or something else) are less important than the total history of God's dealings with and plans for the individual to whom they occur. In Sandy's case we will consider a series of manifestations. She has fallen to the ground many times, trembles fairly frequently, has visions, and has experienced strange power passing through her body. Most strange of all, her stereo once stopped playing music and delivered a message from God. How is it all to be understood? When I met Sandy, I did not encounter an unstable neurotic but a self-effacing, balanced woman with a healthy sense of humor.

God's Pursuit

I met Sandy a couple of years ago. She was a single thirty-seven-year-old woman. She had found Christ almost exactly two years before. Sandy was raised a Methodist but not a particularly religious one. She was baptized as an infant but never understood what grace and the new birth were, which is sad when you remember the life passion of John Wesley, Methodism's founder. Sandy doubts that she was truly a Christian until she "rededicated her life to Jesus Christ" on January 11, 1984.

Sandy's family was middle class and upwardly mobile. As a child she was shy, self-conscious and insecure. But she was also intelligent, perceptive and determined to succeed. She learned to value money, prestige and the perks that came with both by working her way up in the banking world.

Eight years before she found Christ, Sandy met a "real Christian," a fellow student in bank-management training. At that time Sandy's goals were status, financial security and freedom from the restrictions of necessity. But she was more than making do. Her world seemed secure. There was no urgency about religious questions.

Then on April 7, 1981, when she was a local branch manager, matters suddenly changed. Armed men entered the bank to rob it. Into her mouth came the acid taste of life's extreme uncertainty as over a period of several minutes a gun was pointed at the back of her head. The experience changed her life. She began to think seriously about eternity and her spiritual destiny. But fresh promotions followed, driving such thoughts into the background once more. On January 1, 1982, she became an assistant vice president of a major national bank, with duties as a regional financial controller/planner.

Yet God had mercy on her. Almost two years later, on December 26, 1983, while Sandy was at home enjoying a record on her stereo equipment, she was surprised to hear what she thought was static slowly drowning out the music. She wondered what was happening. Could the radio be interfering in some way? Nothing like that had happened before. Then as the music was completely drowned out, the "static" itself stopped, and into the ensuing silence a man's voice said simply and clearly, "Surrender to Jesus!" At once the "static" resumed and then faded until the music from the record came in again. The whole incident could not have lasted more than a minute.

Sandy was so frightened that her heart pounded furiously. Her mind feverishly clung to the idea of radio interference or of some kind of electrical signal superimposed on the record. Had something perhaps happened to the record itself? "I wanted to know if I could duplicate it. . . . I tried a number of times. I played the record over and over. . . ." But there were no repeats. Slowly the realization came to her that the "time had come" for her to resolve her relationship with God.

She struggled against a sense of sinfulness and feelings of un-worthiness "because of my past. . . . Though I wanted to go to heaven I knew it couldn't be, so I . . . just kind of shoved [thoughts of an afterlife] away from me. . . ."

For several days she made no decision but relived the memory of her experience of the voice many times. Her only real access to the Christian world was through television broadcasts. And after work on January 11, 1984, she tuned in to a videotaped program on the Trinity Broadcasting Network. It depicted an evangelistic campaign, currently in progress at Melodyland in Anaheim, California, featuring among other guests the cross-carrying Arthur Blessitt. A conviction gripped her that she should drive that evening across town from her home in West Los Angeles to Anaheim. At the meeting there she "accepted the Lord," an acceptance she perceived at the time as a rededication but that may in fact have represented regeneration.

Assurance amid Confusion

More changes were ahead. The security of her life was to be shaken once again. Major changes were taking place in the bank. The head office was being moved. Three weeks following her conversion she received a notification from the bank that her particular position would end at some point in the near future.

Her conversion had left her happy but confused. Job worries were not her primary concern. Two things disturbed her. She felt unworthy of grace. Had Christ really accepted her? Following her conversion, the major Christian influences on her had been those placing considerable emphasis on experience and on spiritual gifts. As far as she could understand from the television programs she watched, speaking in tongues was of major importance. It was pre-sented as being easy, natural and an essential part of the Christian life. But even after "accepting the Lord" she had not spoken in tongues. Was her conversion real? Had she perhaps not been ac-cepted into the kingdom?

In her mind she proposed a test. For over six months she had suffered mild to moderate pain as a result of a back problem. Pain in the back of her neck radiated to her left shoulder with what she described as a pulling sensation. In addition a persistent ache extended downward to the lower middle part of her back. So one night she prayed for physical healing. She wanted "a sign that he was really listening, that he really cared for me."

God is the God of Gideon and was as gracious to Sandy as to Gideon. She woke about 2:30 A.M. that morning to feel a sensation of heat in the back of her neck, heat that slowly passed downward to the lower lumbar region. The next morning she found that all her pain was gone. She has been free from it ever since. The supernatural origin of the healing was of importance to her only because it assured her that God cared for and accepted her.

More certain now about the reality of her conversion, Sandy joined her parents' Methodist church in March 1984. She also approached her pastor and asked to be baptized. The pastor declined on the grounds that she had already been baptized as an infant. Hurt by what she saw as rejection, she asked him to reconsider. But he felt he should stand by his decision and accept the responsibility of his mistake—if such it should in heaven turn out to be.

As time went on Sandy learned to control the "energy" that first came on her when John and Carol Wimber prayed for her in 1984. While she cannot produce the trembling or the "energy," she can now either resist it or else channel it into prayer even though she was unable to do this at first. Often the trembling would wake her at night or would begin spontaneously during the day. But gradually she learned how to respond more appropriately, and the dramatic nature of the interactions began to subside. In their place came a new sensitivity to the sufferings of others. She might see someone in a shopping mall, sense the person's loneliness and begin to weep. Sickness, confusion or distress in others would provoke a similar reaction at any time or in any place. She wondered, "What is wrong with me? Am I losing my mind?"

Sandy's faith has been tested in many ways. Her father died of cancer, even though she had exercised faith for his healing. She felt the keen winds of criticism blowing from her family and other friends. These stormy trials created bewilderment. But her faith has grown, her understanding has matured and both have become progressively enlightened. "It was a very difficult period for me, but in another sense there was [the feeling that] if no one else cared, he still did." Yet for a while the topics of healing and of her future ministry were topics she did not want to hear about or think about.

Sandy had always been a sensitive person who from her girlhood was uncertain about her personal worth and who tended to withdraw when hurt, internalizing her anger. She did not find it easy to mix and was not assertive. Curiously, and in a Jekyll-and-Hyde fashion, she had been another person professionally. As she advanced through managerial levels in the bank she had learned the persona of her trade and could wear it comfortably. It had given her a feeling of safety and security. She was aware that because she was Black in the essentially White person's world of finance, she was resented. But jealousies and resentment had to be concealed from her. With quiet satisfaction she took her place in a system which obliged people to respond to her role, a role she could play well.

Not that she herself was convinced by the role she played. Indeed her steady advancement was more than a little frightening. She had responded to each offer of advancement with anxious reluctance— which was taken as a covert request for an increase in pay and an advance in title—which would promptly be offered. Eventually she would be pushed up and paid more. In the process, though, she learned to act her part better and better, and she grew sensitive about what her role concealed—the shabbiness of her true nature.

Soon she began to see that God was calling her out of that role to face lack of security, joblessness and rapidly depleting finances. Her job had been her armor. Without it she was forced to see herself in a mirror she did not enjoy looking at. It was an inaccurate mirror, but it was a mirror that had to be looked at before it began to reflect the way God saw her. Only then did she begin to understand more deeply the nature of his grace. Only then was her self-image rebuilt on a more realistic foundation.

She learned by meditating on passages in the Gospels, and she would try to picture vividly the scenes they described. She dreamed vivid dreams and experienced visions. At first, far from being pleased by the visions, she reacted with fear. Yet through them and through her Scripture meditations, and just as powerfully through the unconditional acceptance and love some Christians showed her, she is still experiencing a healing and maturing that goes on and on.

Recovering Self-Worth

Thus in Sandy's life to date, God's work of healing, liberating and equipping has included a wide variety of experiences. It would be foolish to focus on any one aspect (such as the trembling or the being "slain in the Spirit"). None of her experiences can be understood apart from the context of God's entire program for her. However, I will recount one more of her "slayings."

On this occasion, members of the fellowship group she joined decided to pray for one another's future service. When Sandy's turn came they anointed her hands with oil as they prayed. She was only aware enough of their prayers to know that they foresaw some kind of healing ministry for her. But her thoughts were mostly elsewhere, and soon she was aware of a vision.

The world spun in space before her. Ropes from it were wrapped round her waist, tying her to it. From nowhere a hatchet swung down, severing the ropes, which snapped back toward the spinning globe as the Lord pulled her to himself.

She heard group members praying in tongues, felt what she describes as a bolt of energy going through her and fell. As she lay there she was aware continuously of energy passing through her body, but of little else. She knew that the meeting was going on, and that prayer was being made for others. But she felt totally detached.

After what seemed to her like ten or fifteen minutes (actually three and a half hours) she got up. She was unsteady on her feet and was swaying. Things seemed unreal—dreamlike. Someone asked her how she was and she replied, believing that she was replying sensibly. Afterward they told her she had been speaking in tongues. But as her mind recovered its sharp contact with time and space, she became aware of an even greater restoration of her sense of worth—as a child of God. No longer was it dependant on her job or her role in life. This recovery of self-worth has been an enduring one.

Power for Service
Such experiences, though not unique, are far from common for Christians. Sandy presents us with a strange incident in which a stereo seemed to act up, followed later by a conversion, frequent falling on the ground (initially with a rhythmical flailing of limbs), frequent waves of something that felt like electrical power, visions and a progressive restructuring of Sandy's understanding of the nature of her personal worth.

Some people may comment that it all has a pentecostal ring, and having thus classified it, dismiss the story. But naming something only creates the illusion of explaining it. Sandy does not think of herself as pentecostal, even though she gratefully acknowledges the help she received from some pentecostals. Bizarre and unusual events are common in the history of revivals and, as I have already pointed out, in revivals among Calvinists and pentecostals equally.

As we think about the stereo incident, it is important to remember both that Sandy was in a good mood when things began, and that she had no wish for a religious experience. The events do not have a psychological explanation. She did not have a secret wish for a mystical experience. Rather, she was alarmed by what happened, anxiously fiddling with the record player to convince herself that something electronic had gone wrong.

Did something miraculous happen to the stereo? Or was it Sandy's hearing that acted up and not the record player? Of course the real question is: Who made whichever act up? And would it be any more difficult for God to fool with the electronics of stereo systems than with the neurophysiology of hearing? I believe a loving God reached tenderly into the apartment of a needy and rebellious woman and spoke to her. The mechanism he used is unimportant.

And what are we to make of her visions? I have not recorded many of these because of space. None were the result of guided meditation nor of visualization techniques. All were spontaneous. The symbolism conveyed biblical truth powerfully to the points of Sandy's need.

There is also the question of the waves of "tremendous energy" that coursed through her body. Lloyd-Jones, though skeptical about this particular phenomenon, is forced to admit that he is arguing from the silences of Scripture, a form of argument he himself deplores.[1]

Earlier in the book I sought to establish that such experiences in times of revival are not usually "psychological" but represent expressions of God's power. The terms in which various people describe what is happening to them may vary. The general effect is of them being knocked to the ground, and in Sandy's case, this is how it all began. Falls of this sort, accompanied by changes in consciousness, are found in Scripture and history, as discussed in chapter two.

What Sandy experienced when she fell is similar to what Roberts, Finney, Moody, Pascal and many others great and small have experienced. Sandy received anointings of the Spirit's power for future service. The connection of the anointings with sanctification was indirect and incidental. For Sandy the process of healing and sanctification is, as it is for all of us, a long one characterized by leaps of insight and plateaus of integration. Sandy experiences leaps as she grasps—whether through visions, dreams or inductive Bible study (her latest interest)— the wonders of her salvation and of her relationship with the Father.

And the power is increasingly evident in her current Christian service. Sandy's prayers change people's lives. Details of her future service are at this point still unclear. Sandy thinks of herself as in a "holding pattern." But she goes on serving while waiting. And she serves in the manifest power of the Holy Spirit.

14
Conrad: Drugs and a Demon

STIMULATE THE PHAGOCYTES. DRUGS ARE *a delusion."* GEORGE BERNARD SHAW

"And when the demon was driven out, the man who had been mute spoke." MATTHEW 9:33

At the age of twenty-three Conrad, a native of Calgary, Alberta, had already become the administrator of a medium-sized distribution company.[1] His life revolved around parties, sex, drugs, music and money, as it had since he was sixteen. The effort to live a life pure enough to satisfy God had seemed impossibly difficult, and he had put the matter out of his mind.

One day he hired a Christian woman and in the next five years her life and prayers had a profound impact on him. During that time, he also met a former school friend who invited him, along with his wife, to his Bible study group. There he discovered that he didn't have to put God out of his mind. Impossible though it might be to please God, a way had been found. Five years after he hired the Christian employee, both he and his wife discovered that their sins could be pardoned and their lives cleansed.

Breaking an Addiction

A new and profoundly changed life began for them. Instead of the dizzy pursuit of wealth and pleasure, Conrad now attended a Bible study regularly, took his church membership seriously and visited a prison to bear witness to Christ's saving power. But something from the past hung on. Conrad's seventeen-year addiction to marijuana was not broken.

For a while he did not see it as an addiction, even though his wife regularly urged him to stop using it. But in September 1984, God spoke to him clearly. He repented deeply and sorrowfully. But his sorrow did not deliver him. He realized he was trapped. He confessed his sin first to one friend, then to another and finally to his Bible study group, all of whom prayed with him. But in vain. Deliverance did not come. "I simply could not resist temptation," Conrad said. The prayers, the faith and the struggles seemed to avail nothing. But then, he told me:

During this period my friend, Mark, had begun experiencing a new dimension of our Christianity, at least new for our community and church—the power and gifts of the Holy Spirit. He attended a healing conference in Vancouver led by John Wimber and returned home with a new enthusiasm and vision of God's kingdom. He began to pray with new authority and conviction, his teaching became inspired, and God began to use him and others in our community in new . . . ways. Mark told me that some of the same people who had led the Vancouver conference on signs and wonders would be coming to Calgary to lead a miniconference.

Mark encouraged a number of us to attend. I felt God was telling me to go. He had been teaching me something about the role of obedience in the Christian life, and I believe I was being obedient in going, even though I was fearful of what might happen. . . .

Conrad had heard stories of the manifestations that occurred. He had no wish to be a public spectacle by falling on his face, or by coughing, weeping or laughing aloud. But greater than his fear of what might happen was his fear of what might not happen. The contradictory nature of his fears confused him. Would his attendance at the miniconference be another meaningless exercise in faith and prayer? Was there some reason why Conrad would never be delivered from his addiction? And what if he were delivered? How would he manage without his "comforter"?

Both Conrad and Mark find the events of the last Friday in April 1985 hard to explain. Mark, the leader of the meeting Conrad was attending, invited people who wanted prayer to stand. Conrad did not decide to stand and has no recollection of rising to his feet. So he was bewildered to find as he began to look around, that he was out of his seat and standing erect.

A few moments later Conrad saw Ken Blue, a Vineyard leader, and Mark approaching. Confession seemed to pour out spontaneously from him. "Ken, I've been smoking pot for a long time and I want to be free. I want to move on."

Ken faced Conrad. Beside both of them stood Mark, a hand on each of their shoulders. Ken looked at Conrad and said, "In about thirty seconds you will be free." He then prayed, "Father, Conrad hasn't really wanted to be free. Take him now at his word." Manifestations followed, and I shall quote both from Conrad's and from Mark's accounts of what happened. Conrad writes:

As he prayed, I felt an absolutely wonderful, powerful stream of what I best envisage as light pouring in through the back of my neck. I began to shake. . . . I felt a tightness in my chest. It became a convulsion as the power continued to flow in. I began to cough, hack. As this happened the tightness in my chest began to move up through my body and out of my mouth.

This all lasted about two to three minutes. As the tightness left and the convulsing ceased, I felt a void within myself. Ken sensed this and prayed that the void would be filled with God, and it was. I had never experienced such energy in my life, and I had experienced many things. I felt almost drunk, and free and powerful. I knew I had been touched by God and that everything I felt was from him. I knew I had been shown another dimension of God's kingdom on earth. I smiled and felt God's glow for hours.

Conrad had not only convulsed and coughed. His body had arched backward until the upper part of his torso, including his shoulders and his head, seemed to be more or less parallel to the ground. Because his body's center of gravity was no longer above his feet, he should have fallen. But as Ken Blue continued to pray, he remained unsupported in this position as though in the grip of unearthly powers and in defiance of the laws of gravity. Not until a demonic being had left his body did he fall.

Mark's description, both of what he observed and of what he himself experienced, is interesting. It was written two days after the events. "I closed my eyes and began to pray—sort of supporting my other friend [Ken Blue]'s prayer. I started to shake mildly—sort of jerking—not nervous but sort of little spasms." At once Mark was seized by conflicting emotions. What would observers think? That he was super-holy? a weirdo? Firmly he shut such considerations out of his mind, and focused on the importance of what was happening to Conrad, and on his duty to do all he could to help him. "So I said, okay, whatever God wants, he gets!"

At this point it gets weird. I was continuing to affirm the prayers of my friend and I started to lose myself. It's like . . . the tried and true boundaries of my personality slipped away. . . . I sort of fused with my friend [who was] receiving the prayer. I knew—felt, experienced what was going on inside of him. As

[Ken Blue's] prayers got more accurate . . . closer to what the problem was [a spirit] my body went crazy—very powerful jolts, like electricity—and my whole upper body would nod violently in agreement. My spirit would scream inside me, "Yes! Yes!"

As the prayers got very specific and accurate I no longer "heard" them. I experienced them, and a violent struggle between good and evil rose up inside of me. It was awful, like being torn apart. My friends watching me told me later they saw my face sort of screw up in pain and get red, and they thought I would have a heart attack. The struggle was very real and intense, and then [Ken Blue] commanded the spirit to leave.

Instantly [there came] a flood of peace and I knew it was over. Right when the rip happened [Conrad] fell backward and when I turned and opened my eyes he had the biggest smile I've ever seen. He just grinned and said, "It's gone! It's gone! I feel it, it's gone!" He hasn't done drugs since.

Arriving home, Conrad flushed down the toilet all the drugs he had. He was free. Never again would he allow himself to be enslaved. Yet he did "do drugs" once more several weeks after his deliverance. His unbelieving brothers derided and pressed him until for shame he let them overrule him. Instantly he was aware of his folly. Filled with the dread of being caught in the old trap, and with revulsion and an even greater shame, he threw the reefer from him. He has been free and clean since that time.

More importantly, Scripture became alive in a new way, and his times of prayer acquired new meaning and vitality. "What a new life it has been!" he writes. "Not without trials and occasional discouragement, but abundant with joy and encouragement as well. . . . I live in the hope that God will complete the good work he has started in me."

As I watched Conrad across the supper table in a Calgary hotel I knew he was speaking the truth. Nevertheless I later asked his wife, after she had read his written account of what happened, to write me her side of the story. This is what she wrote:

In Conrad's account he mentioned that we had been Christians for some time prior to the powerful working of the Holy Spirit in freeing him from his drug addiction. If I'm honest, I would say that in some respects I thought I was doing a little better than he. . . . I was not using drugs of any kind, though I had in the past. I was also very conscious of trying to create a wholesome home environment for our new infant son and I could not understand why Conrad would not want the same badly enough to simply give up pot. It became apparent, however, that Conrad did want to give up his addiction, and God placed a new attitude in my heart, and I began praying that something would change.

I was quite desperate and did not pray very effectively or at all authoritatively, but God did know what we both wanted—not to mention how badly he would have wanted Conrad free.

I felt very discouraged and arranged to meet Mark. . . . Mark and I had lunch and he, to a certain extent, sensed my selfishness in attitude, and admonished me. We agreed to pray that Conrad would at least tell one other person. Within days, Conrad told our close friend, Chris.

A short while later we attended the healing conference Mark spoke at here in Calgary. Conrad's account describes what happened to him. I was not present when he experienced what he did. . . . I did hear the account of what happened from other friends that were nearby, and that was helpful because I was a little skeptical. I believe God knew that I ought not to be present because of my unbelief.

However, Conrad truly changed!! He was always praying, always reading Scripture. I struggled for a long time with the changes. Even though I wanted him to change, it seemed a little sudden and a little dramatic.

It has been nearly two years and although from time to time I tend to feel left in the dust, I thank God for all he has done and all that I am learning as a result. I am encouraged to walk my own walk with God, which is very good for me. I had a tendency to live the way other Christians . . . thought I should live. There has been a maturity taking place not only in Conrad but also in me.

Long-term Effects

In assessing the reality of manifestations, Jonathan Edwards made it clear that we must look at the spiritual results in the lives of subjects. Conrad did not only enter into a "joy unspeakable and full of glory." He also developed a passion for Scripture and a thirst for prayer. Moreover, he was delivered from a drug addiction that had been resistant to believing prayer, to repentance, to faith, to confession and to tears.

None of these are results the devil would want. All are works of salvation. They attest that the work resulted neither from human emotionalism, from psychology, nor from the works of darkness. They resulted from an encounter between Conrad's body and divine power.

Addictions, whether to sex, drugs, television, gambling, outbursts of rage or to alcohol, constitute a terrible scourge among Christians. We may criticize the victims, blame their lack of faith, their lack of yieldedness, or their insincerity or weakness. But we must also admit a sense of the church's powerlessness in delivering many men and women from these besetting sins, and a sense both of delight and of bewilderment on learning of deliverances like Conrad's. We are delighted to know that God still does things like this but are bewildered that he does not always do it. We cannot understand why so much of our teaching and so many of our prayers do not produce the same dramatic results.

We are dealing, of course, with times of special visitation of the Holy Spirit. What normally should be accomplished by the preaching of the Word, by prayer, by the exercise of true church discipline and by ongoing pastoral care may be accomplished more rapidly and more dramatically in times when revival is near or present.

A Divided Will, a Demonic Presence

Let's look more closely at two aspects of Conrad's dramatic deliverance—the role of his will and the issue of demonic affliction.

Conrad thought he had sought God's help with all his heart and will. He had repented with deep sorrow. His wife was also convinced eventually that he was genuinely trying. ("It became apparent that Conrad . . . did want to give up his addiction. . . .") Nevertheless, Ken Blue, who knew nothing about him, prayed, "Father, Conrad hasn't really wanted to be free," and had urged God to take Conrad's words at face value and to ignore the ambivalence of his heart.

Conrad himself makes it clear that as he faced the prospect of what might happen at the meeting, he made the discovery that his will was divided. "I was afraid," he told me, "not only of what might happen (I had heard the stories of people falling on their faces . . .) but what might not happen. I felt this might be my last hope. I also began to fear the loss of my comforter."

Conrad wanted deliverance, wanted it badly, yet simultaneously he feared to be delivered. Ken Blue's prophetic word was accurate. Conrad had a divided will. Could he expect to be delivered while this was so? Certainly double-mindedness does not normally bring answers to prayer. "That man should not think he will receive anything from the Lord; he is a double-minded man . . ." (Jas 1:7-8). Yet God's grace may do what is neither expected nor deserved.

In this case more than Conrad's imperfect faith and ambivalent will was involved. At the root of his drug addiction lay a demonic affliction, and this raised two more problems. Problem number one: Is there a demon behind every addiction? Problem number two: Can Christians be so afflicted?

There are those who teach that all addictions are demonic, but there is really no way of proving the matter one way or another.

Many addicts, however, are delivered without going through some form of demonic deliverance, and many people who do expose themselves to deliverance ministries are not delivered from the drug, even though a demon has allegedly been cast out. So for practical purposes we must acknowledge that focusing on demons does not always help drug addicts.

In this case, however, it became clear in the course of prayer that a demon was present—in a professing Christian. And at this point many Christians become both indignant and alarmed. Such a state of affairs is surely impossible. How can someone indwelt by the Holy Spirit be afflicted by demons? (Though for that matter, how can someone indwelt by the Holy Spirit entertain sin in the body he occupies? Or more to the point, how could Conrad be utterly under the control of a drug while he was genuinely seeking to yield to an indwelling Holy Spirit?)

Let me begin by dealing with my first caveat. How can someone indwelt by the Holy Spirit entertain sin in the body he, the Spirit, occupies? God cannot look on sin. Sin is utterly repulsive, utterly abhorrent to the Spirit. Yet in mercy and love he continues to dwell in a body where the abhorrent thing is still present.

But are not our sins pardoned? Yes, indeed. But we cling to some of them. We excuse them, cherish them, grieving and quenching the Spirit as we do so. Also in so doing we give our bodies and brains access to the pains and the afflictions demons can render. The only reason they have access to human bodies is that humans are sinful and fallen. Indwelling sin is what gives demons access. It grieves the Spirit. It can provide shelter for a molesting spirit. Only when the Spirit truly fills every part of us are we immune, which is, I believe, the lesson of Matthew 12:43-45 which says, "When an evil spirit comes out of a man, it goes through arid places seeking rest and does not find it. Then it says, 'I will return to the house I left.' When it arrives, it finds the house unoccupied, swept clean and put in order. Then it goes and takes with it seven other spirits more wicked than itself, and they go in and live there. And the final condition of that man is worse than the first."

We talk about "possession" without thinking carefully what this

English word implies, or whether it is the proper word to use. We say possession is nine-tenths of the law! The transliteration of the Greek expression *demon possession* is "demonized." The translation "demon possessed" is, in my view, unfortunate because the word *possessed* is associated in our minds with two things—ownership and total control. When you possess something it is yours. You have the right to do what you want with it.

Christians are not and cannot be owned by demons. They belong to Christ. Nor can they be totally controlled by such beings. Any of us may lose control temporarily and may give way in an unguarded moment to sin and Satan. Others may have "besetting" sins which they seem unable to break. But all of us who are Christ's have come under his dominion, and our aim in life is to bring rebellious areas of our nature under the control of our true master.

If we are to understand what demonized means we must surely look at New Testament descriptions of demonized men and women. As we examine them, I think you will agree that most would better be described as men and women afflicted by demons rather than owned and totally controlled by them. Afflicted in and through their bodies to be sure. Hence the need for the demons to be driven out. But the demons do not own the bodies of Christians.

In many cases there is no clear description, but in several instances there is. The Gadarene demoniac alone might come under the category of someone owned and totally controlled by demons. And yet even in his case the description is not necessarily true. Self-control and demon-control seem to alternate in the man. Under his own control he runs to Jesus and falls at his feet. The act looks like an act of worship. But the demon within him then cried, "What do you want with me, Jesus, Son of the Most High God?" (Mk 5:6-7).

But take the case of the epileptic boy at the foot of the Mount of Transfiguration. He was afflicted with periodic fits of epilepsy. When Jesus cast the demon out the boy was healed (Mt 17:18). You can be healed of an affliction, not of a possession. The account of the same incident in Mark is yet more graphic. Here the spirit is described as one of deaf mutism—certainly an affliction from which any of us would wish to be healed (Mk 9:14-27).

Again, the Canaanite woman who came to Jesus on behalf of her demonized daughter said that her daughter was "suffering terribly" from her demonization (Mt 15:22). The expression suggests affliction, pain, torment. Moreover when Jesus grants her request we are told that her daughter, like the epileptic boy, was healed. The word *healed* is used of a bodily affliction, and is comparable more with a sickness a demon causes than with an ownership to which the spirit has no right, even in the unconverted.

Conrad was, I believe, afflicted by a demon. The demonic affliction took the form of an addiction to drugs. It may well have attached itself to Conrad's body at some point during his abuse of drugs, and in this sense Conrad deserved what he got. Unfortunately, though deliverance from many sins follows confession and faith, the matter is less simple when a demonic presence is involved. The abuse had provided an opportunity for demonic attachment of some kind. Not until Ken Blue, under the authority of the kingdom of God and in the power of the Spirit, served notice to the demon was the matter resolved.

What of the Other Strange Manifestations?
What was the meaning of Conrad's "light pouring in through the back of my neck"? The symbolism is pleasing—light to overcome his inner darkness. I have no idea why the back of his neck should be the portal of entry, but grace does not seem to be choosy. Obviously, Conrad was having an experience that we cannot share, and he gropes to make us understand what he felt. It was not light, but in Conrad's own words "what I best envisage as light. . . ."

Experiences of this sort are never easy to communicate. Often they can only be communicated approximately and by imperfect analogies. In Scripture, too, there is an "as it were" quality about the visions, say, of Ezekiel or John. But what is observed by onlookers, in contrast, is easy to describe, though not always to understand. What are we to make of the arching of Conrad's back? Although I did not describe it in chapter seven where I confined myself to the commonest manifestations, I have come across several reliable reports of people bending so far back that their heads touch the ground behind them. In most cases I have heard reported, demons were not involved. A powerful work of the Spirit was being done involving a significant life change.

Two of the cases I learned of were in older people, who presumably had arthritic problems in their vertebral columns. Nevertheless, they were capable of a contortion most of us could never reproduce, and curiously suffered no adverse physical aftereffects. I have no explanation for what happened to Conrad, other than to say that when a human body comes into immediate contact with divine power, physical changes occur. And the greater the power, the more dramatic may be the changes.

Mark's strange identification with Conrad makes him sound like Mr. Spock in a Vulcan mind meld. The crisis began for Mark when he said to himself, "Whatever God wants, he gets." The power of the Holy Spirit was resting on him at that point, just as it rested on the other two. As a result he was temporarily able to "see" or to experience what was happening to Conrad, both in his body and in his spirit, and almost as clearly as if it were happening to himself. However, he did not, as the fictitious Mr. Spock does, fuse his identity with someone else to achieve this, even if it felt to Mark something like that. Rather he saw and felt with prophetic vision or insight. And since the conflict in Conrad was intense, Mark experienced it intensely.

We could compare it, in a small degree, to the way God himself experiences our pain. He told Moses, "I have seen the affliction of my people who are in Egypt. . . . I know their sufferings" (Ex 3:7 RSV). The word *know* means more than having an intellectual grasp of the situation. In Hebrew it means a deep personal involvement. Later when Israel was oppressed by foreigners, the writer of the book of Judges tells us that the Lord "could bear Israel's misery no longer" (10:16). Likewise the Lord asked Paul, "Why do you persecute me?" (Acts 9:4) indicating that he suffers when his people suffer. No opaque walls hide our bodily and spiritual experiences from God.

What Mark went through was understandably bewildering. If the walls that now separate us from one another suddenly were to become invisible, so that we could experience what everyone else experienced as clearly as we experience ourselves, we would be frightened and disoriented. We are not used to it. Mark's experience was the experience of a man blind from birth seeing for the first time.

I have seen the same thing happening in my family. I remember my mother suddenly turning round sharply at home and with a startled expression on her face, saying, "Your Auntie Jenny's having an operation! They're anesthetizing her. I can smell the chloroform!" And it was so. At that hour. My mother was not a psychic. So far as I know it was the only time something like that ever happened to her. And she did what a Christian does under those circumstances. She prayed for the person whose chloroforming she could smell.

In a similar way my grandmother was aroused from sleep one night during the Battle of the Somme in World War 1 to see my Uncle John, her son, marching wearily in his muddied uniform, beside her bed. Suddenly he clutched his belly and pitched head-first through the floor. She waited months for the cable from the war office, knowing what it would say, ". . . missing in action and presumed dead." His sergeant later visited her and described to her exactly what she had seen.

Many Christians have these experiences. Some fear to talk about them because they go under the rubric of second sight and are thought to be occult. And so they can be. They are in fact brief flashes of prophetic insight. And as I continue to insist, people can have such experiences in alliance with the powers of darkness even

WHEN THE SPIRIT COMES WITH POWER ◆

though in their origins they are God-given. But in Mark's case, as in the case of my mother and my grandmother, the thing was unsought and God-given, and for a merciful and gracious purpose. The results were certainly from God in Conrad's case. And in mercy God did not allow him to slip in spite of his one brief relapse. But we must be warned. Deliverance, though real, does not render us immune to demonic affliction. But Ken Blue had the wisdom to ask the Holy Spirit to fill the space the demon had vacated, and his prayer was immediately answered. For that reason the Holy Spirit in his faithfulness had delivered Conrad in the hour of temptation. There was further temptation, and even sin when his brothers goaded him into smoking another reefer. But sensitive to the Spirit's control, Conrad had reacted with revulsion and fear to what happened, and sin had not led to bondage. Had he grieved the Spirit by ignoring him, Conrad would have opened the way to a worse condition.

Adjustments for Both Husband and Wife
His wife's comments are interesting. Wives have a struggle when addicted husbands are delivered from their addiction, and one senses a little of that struggle in her brief comments, loyal as she is. She states, "I struggled for a long time with the changes. Even though I wanted him to change, it seemed a little sudden and a little dramatic." Two years later she was still feeling as though she were left behind in the dust.

Within marriage different patterns begin to emerge after deliverance of one partner from alcohol or drugs. The new patterns demand adjustments. And at that point the adjustments are frequently much tougher on the nonaddicted spouse than on the delivered spouse. Suddenly you find yourself living with a different person. Things differ markedly from what the nonaddicted spouse may have for years been anticipating.

But in Conrad's case, his wife knew that what happened was God's doing. God had not finished with Conrad, but God had begun. And Conrad's wife makes two more interesting comments. Regarding his deliverance she says, "I believe God knew that I ought not to be present because of my unbelief." And of her adjustments she says, "I thank God for all he has done and all that I am learning as a result. I am encouraged to walk my own walk with God, which is very good for me. I had a tendency to live the way other Christians . . . thought I should live. There has been a maturity taking place not only in Conrad but also in me."

I believe the two comments are related. They reveal not only her spiritual maturity, but her preparation for a further work of the Holy Spirit in her own life. Unbelief is often related to our need to live as other Christians think we should, to be glancing at ourselves constantly in the mirror of social approval. God's work is hindered often by that need. We must determine to lay it aside as we await his further work in our hearts.

15
Jim:
Power
Encounter

I HAD NO STRENGTH LEFT, MY FACE TURNED
*deathly pale and I was helpless. Then I heard him speaking, and as I
listened to him, I fell into a deep sleep, my face to the ground."* DANIEL
THE PROPHET

Jim Hylton pastors a large Baptist church in Fort Worth, Texas.
He told me his story when we first met in California and later
supplied me with a written record of it.[1]
Early in my ministry as a pastor [at a time when the author had
been completely convinced that there were no demons] an in-
satiable hunger to know the Lord intimately began to occur.
That pilgrimage led eventually to the First Baptist Church, West
Plains, Missouri, to be a pastor. In that church was a former

missionary to China, Dr. Jeanette Beale. Her description of one of the greatest manifestations of God's power in revival furthered and intensified my quest.

In October 1966, the power of God descended upon the service, and we did not leave the service until early afternoon. In that divine invasion I was moved experientially far beyond my understanding. Only the grace of God kept us on course.

One of the ladies in the church was angered by the change she had seen occur in my life. One morning after a service she exploded, "I hate you. All you want to talk about is Jesus. You were such a good preacher. I am sick and tired of all this Jesus talk." The wellspring of joy that flowed in me caused me to laugh a lot even when I was preaching. My response was to laugh. Her response was to wheel around and hurry away.

The next week she came to the study. It was apparent she was no longer angry but broken and apologetic. Her face showed she had lost sleep and experienced much anguish. She wept as she said, "I am sorry for what I said Sunday. You see the reason I can't stand you speaking about Jesus is because all the sin I have committed brings much anguish to my heart."

I knew little about supernatural power beyond the most supernatural expression of all, the new birth. The Lord knew I was totally incapable to deal with her problem. He simply took me out of it. As I sat in the high-backed chair behind my desk I was suddenly so overwhelmed by the power of the Lord I could no longer hear. I tried to move and found myself plastered to the chair unable to move a muscle. I could see her and knew she was talking but couldn't hear a word. My first thought was I was dying and with the Lord's presence everything else was fading out.

She looked intently, sensing the Lord's power upon me. Then she hurriedly ran out of the side exit of the study. As the Lord's power pressed me into the chair I couldn't move. I sat there reflecting on what was happening and what I ought to do about it if I could. My mind was saying, "I've counseled with many people and this never happened, Lord. Help me." The intensity of power began to lessen and I heard in my spirit, "Go after her."

I found her in the auditorium weeping out her heart before the Lord as she repented of every sin he showed her. After she regained some composure I told her I was sorry she was frightened, but I could not explain what was happening. She said, "I understand. It was the glory of the Lord I saw on your face, and I couldn't stand to be there."

We returned to the study, and I sat down in the same chair and was gone again. The power of God came on me until I was barely able even to see this time and could not hear at all. I could see as she fell into the carpet of the study. After a time which I have no way to measure, she rose to her chair with the glory of God on her. She sat for a long time looking into space saying nothing. My own senses returned to normal, and she looked into my face with a great relief and said, "Demons have gone out of me." A man who didn't even believe in demons had to be taken clear out of the play. For years I never told that story. I never understood it for one thing. Only in the last year as I have seen people go into unconsciousness when the power of God comes on them have I understood what God was doing to me that day.

The Power Encounter

A number of points in Jim's story call for comment. All of them have to do with the expulsion of demons. The expulsion was preceded not only by a deep conviction of sin, a conviction arising from the Spirit's overwhelming presence, but by broken confession. It was an expulsion that took place without any human intervention. After all, Jim didn't believe in demons. It was also a demon expulsion involving the woman being thrown on the ground. And finally, it was an expulsion evidenced by the fact that beforehand the woman had been unable to remain in Jim's presence because she had seen the glory of the Lord in his face.

Jim's own explanation of this bizarre series of events is that God took him out of action. God did this, Jim supposes, because he did not believe in demons and would have been unlikely to try to cast them out of a lady whose problem was demonic. He could be right. Had the lady been willing to receive his counsel he might have spent hours in dealing with her and been totally ineffective. Instead, in two dramatic encounters, Jim had been taught a lesson and a woman's life had been revolutionized. The lesson was a bizarre and dramatic lesson in everyday, practical demonology.

The demonic expulsion took the form of what is known as a power encounter. In part one, I referred to the two most dramatic power encounters in the Old Testament—the encounter in which Moses shamed the magicians of Egypt and the power encounter in which Elijah, in a clash with Baal's prophets, demonstrated to the Israelites that the true God was not Baal but Yahweh. I made it clear that Satan's power, having (like Satan himself) its origin in heaven, is often indistinguishable from God's power in its manifestations. However, when the two come into conflict, a power encounter ensues. Inevitably the greater overthrows the lesser, the infinite always proving stronger than the finite, the source than that which is derived from it.

Some scholars feel that Christ's supreme power over the storm was a power encounter. They point out that the storm occurred when he and the disciples were on their way to the Garasenes. The expulsion of a legion of demons would be a critical turning point in the assertion of his messiahship, and they see the winds and waves as being lashed into fury unnaturally by demonic forces. In that incident the storm had dashed itself uselessly against the eternal rock. At his word of rebuke demon hordes fled in terror. The howling wind sank into cowed submission, and the tempestuous waves flattened themselves in fear.

In Jim's case, two more points about the demon expulsion are important. The woman fell to the ground. Some people may fall from hysteria or the desire to be part of a mass movement. Her fall was not the result of mass hysteria since she was alone with a pastor who was incapacitated in his chair. Moreover, she was opposed to behavior of that sort. She was affected in a way similar to the boy out of whom Jesus cast a demon in Mark 9.

More interesting still, she apparently did not know she had any demons, and possibly didn't even believe in their existence. Yet immediately following the experience she herself stated, "Demons have gone out of me." She had an instantaneous and clear-cut understanding of what had happened to her, the result of spiritual illumination. I have dealt directly with two similar cases in the past three years.

An Immobilized Body, a Shining Face
Many aspects of Jim's story defy rational explanation. Why did God need to incapacitate Jim? Could he not have revealed the true state of affairs in a less dramatic way? If Jim were at that point walking in an intimate relationship with the Lord, would it not seem more natural for God to have rebuked his servant's prejudice about demons? Again, why did the power of God continue to press Jim into the chair for some time after the woman left him?

God is sovereign. If he chooses not to explain all his reasons to us or to be dramatic in the way he goes about things, who are we to question? The God of the still small voice is sometimes the God of fire and tempest. He does whatever he wants in heaven and on earth. And if we are puzzled about Jim's continuing difficulty in the chair, let us remember that Daniel was ill for weeks after one encounter with the supernatural.

For the woman the problem had begun with Jim's joyful obsession with Jesus following his revival experience. She could not stand the change in his preaching. To her it was a "savor of death unto death." She told him, "You see the reason I can't stand you speaking about Jesus is because all the sin I have committed brings much anguish to my heart."

The theme irritated her. It was Christ-centered. More importantly, there was a power in Jim's preaching that had not been present
previously. Christ-centered content is not automatically empowered. (People who preached Moody's sermons verbatim, using his
mannerisms and inflections, never got Moody's results!) The demons within the woman who confronted Jim recognized the
change—and the new power in his preaching. They would have
remained quiet had Jim's preaching not been empowered. But like
the judges and the prophets in the Old Testament and the disciples
in the New Testament, like Wesley, Whitefield, Finney, Torrey
and Moody, Jim had received an anointing of divine power which
had changed his ministry significantly. Some Christians might be
unimpressed, but the woman's demons knew. Jim was now a threat
to them.

And the profound conviction of sin that drove the woman to
distraction was not the result of emotional hellfire preaching. The
sermons were preached by a man whose mouth was filled with
laughter. Her conviction was the same type that occurred on the
day of Pentecost, a result of the powerful presence of the Holy
Spirit. Her broken confession was important in and of itself. But
it may also have had a bearing on the demon expulsion. People
experienced in deliverance often comment that there are times
when resistant demons will not leave where the subject is still
hanging on to some specific sin.

In chapter seven I discussed holy laughter, the strange release
from tension that some people experience, a wonderful thing when
it is truly of the Spirit, but something that grates on even the
observers when it is mimicked. Jim comments that he found himself laughing more than he had done previously. Laughter sparkled
through his sermons. Instead of grappling with angry feelings at the
woman's expression of hatred, he had burst out with laughter.

Over the years the tendency to laugh has been tempered somewhat in Jim, whose joy is accompanied by gravity. He also is now
fully aware of the presence of demons and has experience in casting

them out. But it can truly be said that the empowering in his ministry has not left him.

The final point about the power encounter has to do with the glory on Jim's face, a glory of which he was unaware, but that drove the demonized woman in terror from his presence. "It was the glory of the Lord I saw on your face, and I couldn't stand to be there." An even greater glory shone from Moses' face. "Moses . . . was not aware that his face was radiant. . . . They were afraid to come near him" (Ex 34:29-30). It shone like the transfigured Jesus (Mk 9:2-3) and like Stephen before his martyrdom. (The Sanhedrin had no excuse for their crime in condemning Stephen to death, for Acts 6:15 tells us they "looked intently at Stephen, and they saw that his face was like the face of an angel.")

Similar manifestations have occurred throughout church history. A recent one is reported by Lloyd-Jones, to whom a woman converted in the Hebrides revival (to which I referred in chapter two) told her story. Apparently she was little interested in the revival but was eventually persuaded to attend one of the house meetings. Lloyd-Jones tells us, "She failed to get in once or twice because of the crowd but eventually succeeded. . . . And the thing that led to her conversion was the sight of the face of a little girl in that house. The woman suddenly saw the face of this child shining, and that was the means of her conviction of sin, her need of a Saviour, her salvation and her being filled with the Holy Spirit."[2]

The glory on Jim's face was not Jim's glory, but God's.

Part III
When the Spirit Comes with Power

16
Preparing
for Revival

IN THIS BOOK I HAVE LOOKED AT TWO closely related questions: Are the manifestations I have examined a sign that another revival may be on the way? More importantly: Are they from God? I have concluded that in the recent past most of them seem to be manifestations of the Holy Spirit's power. I also conclude that a major revival could be on the way. The question then arises: What ought we to do?

The Work of Persistent Prayer
We should do a number of things. We should tell the Christian public what God has done in past revivals without sentimentalizing the stories. We must point to human failure and sin in the story,

to human stupidities and mistakes, as well as to the glories of Christ's triumphs. We should teach churches the errors to watch out for as well as the blessings to anticipate. But while we are doing this, we must not so frighten people by the negatives that we scare them away from the glory. For revival is what we desperately need. And it is God's delight to send it.

Above all, we must pray. Indeed we must give ourselves to earnest and persistent prayer. What we term renewal is not enough. Dramatic evidences of divine power are of no importance in themselves. If renewal within the church is to fulfill God's purpose for it and if Christ is to be glorified, it must lead to a major evangelistic thrust. It must result in what was once called an awakening in society generally. Only an extraordinary outpouring of God's Spirit will accomplish that.

The awakening must also lead to reforms in society. In the Great Awakening when large numbers were truly born from above, they did more than join churches. By their prayers, their radically changed outlook, their obedience and their example, they changed British society profoundly. A climate emerged in which legislative and political changes followed, and followed in a way that could and would not ever have been achieved by political activism alone. The changes were a sort of spin-off from the outpouring of divine power.

We must therefore plead for an outpouring of the Holy Spirit on Christian congregations. This seems to be what God would like to give us. We are called to collaborate with him in prayer that it may happen. And in praying for such an outpouring we must, if we are consistent, pray that the Spirit may be poured out upon each one of us personally. What I ask for the church and for society, I must ask for myself.

My prayers must not, however, be self-seeking. There must be no hidden agenda in my traffic with God. Do I secretly long for an esoteric experience? To seek it will not only be wrong but could be dangerous. Do I long for power and gifts that will elevate me above my fellow Christians? Gifts and power are one thing, but elevation above my fellow Christians is quite another. My desire must be both for God himself and for an empowering that will enable me to serve him.

It is one thing for me to urge persistent prayer for either personal or corporate revival, and quite another for anyone to pray with faithful and unwavering faith. How do you get from being a discouraged intercessor to a warrior who prevails in prayer?

How in particular does one acquire the sort of faith that casts mountains into the sea? To pray for a revival to sweep the land is much more significant, demands a far greater exercise of power than merely tossing Mount Everest into the Indian Ocean. Yet Jesus talks about such feats as though the prayers that occasion them were the heritage of all God's children.

"Have faith in God. . . . I tell you the truth, if anyone says to this mountain, 'Go, throw yourself into the sea,' and does not doubt in his heart but believes that what he says will happen, it will be done for him. Therefore I tell you, whatever you ask for in prayer, believe that you have received it, and it will be yours" (Mk 11:22-24).

Andrew Murray comments on the key to our difficulty—our difficulty in finding sufficient faith and persistence within ourselves to pray this way. As he examines Mark 11:22-24, he notes that what seem to be Christ's impossibly wild, almost irresponsible claims about the prayer of faith are preceded by the words, "Have faith in God." Faith in God comes before faith in the promise.

Faith in the promise, he tells us, must be an outgrowth of faith in the promiser. You cannot have total, unwavering faith that something will come to pass unless you have come to know Someone well enough to trust him and to know what he wants. Intimacy with a person is involved. The more intimately you know him, the more confidence you have in him, the more clearly you see and hear him. And by the very tone of his voice you know that what he says is true. As Murray puts it, ". . . faith is the ear by which

I hear what is promised, the eye by which I see."[1]

Yet is not this the very reason we were saved? Was not Paul's main ambition that of knowing Christ? But would not such a profound and intimate knowledge of God demand that I inhabit rarefied spiritual atmosphere, that I enjoy an ongoing mountaintop existence?

The last question is the wrong question. We still do not understand the Father's heart. We say there is nothing that would delight us more than intimacy with him, implying as we protest, that such a degree of intimacy is beyond us. What we forget is that the Father wants it more than we do. He longs for it. He sacrificed his only Son to make it possible. Therefore he will go more than the second mile with anyone who shares that same longing.

What is the Father like? Jesus described him in Luke 15. He is the father who waits on the rooftop daily for years, straining his eyes at the horizon. (How else would he have spotted the prodigal "while he was still a long way off" if not from a rooftop—Lk 15:20?) No, the Father is the father who tore out of the house shouting instructions for a feast to the servants, stumbling blindly toward the boy his arms longed to embrace. He is the father who even stifled the speech of repentance halfway through as he cried out for a new robe and a ring for the boy's finger. And this Father feels the same way about you and me when we set out to meet him from a distance.

He wants us all to know him as "Abba." When you know him like that your faith will be simpler and clearer, your prayers at once reverent, intimate, informed. You will know what he wants you to ask, and you will want it because he does. You will hear his promises in his very commands, and in the smile with which he lights up your heart.

Did you ever try to call him Daddy? If you're like me you'll find it very difficult. Why? For many reasons. It sounds as though it lacks respect. Yet a child uses the expression without a thought—which is just the point. You see we are talking about becoming little children before the Father. Some of us have grown up saying "Daddy" to our fathers, and as we have grown to maturity (and some of our parents to senility) the word *Daddy* has expressed a slightly patronizing, but tolerant endearment—an attitude and posture utterly incompatible with our relationship with the Father of Lights.

He is not "dear old Dad" but the daddy seen through the trusting, adoring eyes of a little child. It is not easy to become a little child. Simplicity comes hard. But if intimacy and power are what we want we must become helpless little children who know him as Daddy.

Yet since he himself craves this intimacy with us, it should not be thought of as an impossible achievement. Only our carnal sort of dignity must go and a humble trust be added. It will seem odd at first. Difficulties there may be, but if God be for us, who can be against us?

I can think of two books that are helpful for anyone interested in pursuing this further. The first is one I have already referred— Andrew Murray's *With Christ in the School of Prayer*. The other is *The Joy of Listening to God* by Joyce Huggett.[2] Murray's book deals with the secrets of intercession by one who was intimate with the Father. Huggett's is full of practical suggestions about waiting quietly in the Lord's presence.

Is there anything of greater worth in this life than to know him?

The Indwelling and Quickening Spirit

What does Scripture have to say about such an empowering? For the last eighty years (indeed since the holiness views both of John Wesley and John Fletcher of Madely), the answer has been obscured by the heated controversy over the baptism of the Holy Spirit. Let us examine the question briefly, as far as possible without alluding to the controversy itself.

One major difficulty is conceptualizing the Holy Spirit's relationship with us as believers. Our bodies have a certain volume. We are temporal and dimensional beings who, because we have not experienced eternity, have difficulty understanding what eternity is.

God, on the other hand, inhabits eternity. He is spirit. In one sense he does not occupy any space—that is to say he does not, like us, have a specific volume that can be measured. In another sense, of course, he fills all space. If you are a Christian, the nonspatial Holy Spirit indwells you, may even fill you. Since he is a person we could say that all of him is inside your body. (You can't have only part of a person inside your body.) Yet I and every other Christian have all of him too. In him we all become one, yet without losing our individual identities. But such ideas can be confusing if we think of an infinite person being "crammed into" each one of our little bodies. We conceive of ourselves as separate from one another, largely because we occupy separate chunks of space.

Since we automatically think in spatial and temporal terms, we must be careful as we look at the terms the Bible uses in describing the Spirit's operations in and upon us. Indeed the two little words *in* and *on* generally relate to two distinct aspects of what the Holy Spirit does for God's people. He is in all of us all the time. He comes on us for specific purposes at certain times. When he comes on us he is sometimes said to fill us. And though it may seem confusing to us that he could come on or upon someone he already lives inside, the confusion has to do with our inability to think in anything but spacial terms. Prepositions are helpful, and the Scripture uses them, but we must try to use the terms just as the Scripture does, without letting spatial concepts confuse us too much.

Even in the Old Testament the Holy Spirit is described as dwelling in certain people. Some scholars deny this. But Peter seems quite clear on the matter, referring to the way in which "the prophets . . . searched intently . . . trying to find out the time and circumstances to which the Spirit of Christ in them was pointing . . ." (1 Pet 1:10-11). Pharaoh referred to Joseph as "one in whom is the spirit of God" (Gen 41:38). Not being a follower of the true God he might not have known what he was talking about.

But God told Moses about Bezalel, "See, I have chosen Bezalel son of Uri, the son of Hur, of the tribe of Judah, and I have filled him with the Spirit of God . . ." (Ex 31:2). God later said to Moses, "Take Joshua son of Nun, a man in whom is the spirit . . ." (Num 27:18). David asked God not to remove the Holy Spirit from him (Ps 51:11).

But the indwelling of the Spirit in the Old Testament was only an exceptional anticipation of a more general blessing to be realized in the New. That is what Ezekiel referred to when he prophesied, "And I will put my Spirit in you and move you to follow my decrees . . ." (Ezek 36:27), or again, "I will put my Spirit in you and you will live . . ." (Ezek 37:14).

For in the New Testament the indwelling Spirit was to give all believers the authority to be called sons and daughters of the living God, sanctifying, guiding and instructing them as they were given a new life that took the fear of death and mortality away.

All believers, from the moment of their conversion, are indwelt in this way. The indwelling both defines the status of believers and gives them immortality. As Paul puts it, "If anyone does not have the Spirit of Christ, he does not belong to Christ. . . . And if the Spirit of him who raised Jesus from the dead is living in you, he who raised Christ from the dead will also give life to your mortal bodies through his Spirit, who lives in you" (Rom 8:9-11). In this sense all of us are jointly and individually God's temple (1 Cor 3:16).

The Empowering and Enabling Spirit

But we are not only indwelt and made alive by the Holy Spirit. We are equipped by him to work in his kingdom and to conquer the dark powers as soldiers of Christ. In general the Bible uses the preposition *on* or *upon* to describe the way in which he gives us this power. And the references to this exceed in number even those that have to do with his indwelling.

The Spirit rests on or upon people when this happens (Is 11:2).

He is shed on or upon; he comes on; he is poured on; he is poured out on or upon them (1 Sam 10:6; 19:20, 23; Is 32:15; Ezek 39:29; Joel 2:28-29; Zech 12:10; Acts 2:33; 10:44). The term *filled with* also seems usually to refer to this empowering or enabling. In Exodus 31:3, you may remember, Bezalel was enabled to do skilled work because he was filled with the Spirit. Micah was empowered as the Spirit filled him. "But as for me, I am filled with power, with the Spirit of the LORD . . ." (Mic 3:8). As Zechariah reminds us, God's work is done "not by might nor by power, but by my Spirit" (Zech 4:6).

The Spirit comes upon men and women to enable them to do all the work of the kingdom. Isaiah predicted the day when God would "pour water on the thirsty land, and streams on the dry ground" and would pour out his Spirit "on your offspring . . ." (Is 44:3). The Spirit was to be upon the anointed Servant, to enable him to accomplish the many tasks of the kingdom, "The Spirit of the Sovereign LORD is on me, because the LORD has anointed me to preach good news . . . bind up . . . proclaim freedom . . ." and more (Is 61:1-2).

Unlike the indwelling of the Spirit, which automatically follows repentance and true faith in Christ, empowerings and infillings may occur once or many times, at conversion or subsequent to conversion. King Saul, you may remember, is described as having the Holy Spirit come upon him on two occasions. On one he prophesied and was honored (1 Sam 10:10-11), but on the other he was humiliated and forced to prophesy against his will (1 Sam 19:23-24).

In many instances the "coming upon" is entirely at the Holy Spirit's initiative, and not in response to a request by the person on whom he falls. It is, as Lloyd-Jones puts it, "something that happens to you." Certainly this was true in Saul's case. However, the person is usually obeying God when the incident occurs, and in any case we are encouraged to ask for this gift of God. It would be unwise to press the differences too far, but whereas the indwelling never changes, the effects of the anointing, or empowering, seem often to fade. Why otherwise would it be repeated?

The disciples could have been indwelt by the Holy Spirit before Pentecost. Several weeks before, the risen Jesus had appeared to them and had breathed on them saying, "Receive the Holy Spirit. If you forgive anyone his sins, they are forgiven; if you do not forgive them, they are not forgiven" (Jn 20:22-23). Nearly three hundred years ago Matthew Henry, commenting on the same verse, arrived at the conclusion that it was the point at which the Spirit began to indwell all believers. "What Christ said to them, he says to all true believers, 'Receive ye the Holy Ghost.' "[3]

Lloyd-Jones argues for the traditional, as opposed to the commoner, current interpretations of the passage which suggest that nothing significant happened in John 20. Jesus was merely "enacting beforehand" an event which would be realized at Pentecost. The traditional view, on the other hand, maintained that at that point (and not on the day of Pentecost) the church came into being. How can the issue be resolved?

Perhaps it cannot entirely be resolved. But the real issue seems to be that anointings, empowerings, "comings upon" and the like differ from and must not be confused with that ongoing indwelling that begins with the new birth. They may coincide with the new birth (see Acts 11:15), or they may follow it. They may occur once or many times, or perhaps not at all. If the disciples were indwelt for the first time at Pentecost, the Spirit's coming to dwell does not seem to be the only thing that happened. The tongues of flame empowered them in a way the church in North America is not empowered.

So what happened at Pentecost? A group of believers who may or may not already have been indwelt by the life-giving and sanctifying Spirit, were "clothed with power from on high." I do not know why they had to wait. Why do delays occur? Often they don't. Some are clothed with power at their conversion. But at Pentecost flames "came to rest on" the disciples, enabling them to speak in other tongues. Commonly conversion is a quiet affair, but their being clothed with power was noisy and dramatic, and its effects attracted a lot of attention.

Following Pentecost there were subsequent outpourings on and infillings affecting the believers. We could call some of them minor. Certainly nothing the Spirit does is of minor importance, but some anointings have major and more widespread effects. The greater the outpouring, the noisier and more dramatic it seems to have been. Peter had commanded a well-known cripple to stand on his feet. The healing created a sensation, and Peter used the opportunity to proclaim Jesus as Messiah. Peter and John were arrested.

At their trial Peter, under a special anointing of the Holy Spirit, astounded the Sanhedrin by his bold and eloquent defense (Acts 4:8, 13). Let us, for the sake of clarity, call the anointing he had received a *minor* anointing or event, to distinguish it from the *major* event that followed.

Subsequently, unable to take any effective action, the Sanhedrin threatened Peter and John and released them. They could not oppose the miracle, but they were to stop claiming that Jesus was behind it (Acts 4:16-17). There was to be no more preaching in the name of Jesus! How did the church respond in the face of the threats?

Indignantly they came before God in prayer and requested boldness to go on preaching, and more signs and wonders to back the preaching up (Acts 4:29-30). In response there came an outpouring of power that shook the building and produced a renewed equipping of everyone present. We could refer to it as a major outpouring or event, thus distinguishing it from what happened to Peter.

But the distinction has to do with size only. The theological significance is the same in both instances. The disciples were promptly filled once again with the Holy Spirit. This in turn gave them boldness in the face of danger, unity and indifference to personal wealth (Acts 4:32-37) and the ability to perform more miraculous signs (Acts 5:1-16).

That second outpouring of the Spirit in response to prayer was a major turning point in the church's history. It was a point at which they could have backed down and sunk into oblivion instead of going forward. Yet how could they go forward? As a group of poorly organized, ignorant and politically unsophisticated men and women, how could they counter the powerful foes arrayed against them? What in fact they did was to request power from above. And power was poured out on them. Faced with supernatural boldness and new displays of power (including an angelic intervention), the chief priests were furious and contemplated the deaths of the apostles. However, at Gamaliel's advice the newly arrested apostles were again released. Preaching continued and the church, far from fading away, continued to grow in maturity and effectiveness (Acts 5:41-42).

Downpours and Droughts
This earnest cry to God in prayer at a critical point in the church's history had incredible results. It is time to prove God again. But let me be clear that anointings such as Peter's occur frequently even when revival is not present. They occur to all Christians irrespective of their theological convictions, and whether or not they understand the nature of what is happening. The Holy Spirit in this way anoints (or falls on) charismatics and anti-charismatics, in times of renewal and in "ordinary" times.

What ministers of any theological stripe have not had the repeated experience of facing a congregation with the realization that he or she has nothing to give? How many of us have been empty of anything but the lifeless outline of an address, have been weary in mind and body, have sensed no fellowship with God—until the very moment when we opened our mouths? How many of us under those circumstances have been astonished both by the joy and the free flow of living insights? Only when our address was over did we return to our emptiness. Such experiences go beyond what psychological laws can explain. The Holy Spirit rested on us while we preached. And let me repeat it—these incidents had nothing to do with our particular views on how operations of the Holy Spirit are supposed to work.

As a conservative evangelical I always called my moments of prophetic insight hunches and intuitions, recognizing only in retrospect and after many years that the insights had in fact resulted from the Spirit's gently coming upon me. In pastoral prayers I would sometimes find myself caught up beyond ordinary prayer as I was momentarily stunned by a vision of what might be. I would be shocked at the bold words I was pouring out. Quickly I would suppress what was happening lest my tongue should run away with me. Yet years later, knowing that God had been speaking, people would quote the very words I uttered during those moments, remembering the powerful impressions the words conveyed. In my concern for a reputation of sobriety, I had repeatedly quenched the Spirit.

During times of revival such anointings seem to be both more frequent and more powerful. Major outpourings occur and minor anointings become ten-a-penny. Prayer flows more easily. Preaching is more powerful. Guidance is more vivid. In contrast at other times we learn the tougher lessons of walking by naked faith in the Word. This may partly explain why times of revival alternate with times of spiritual drought. Certainly we learn lessons in drought that could never be learned in a cloudburst. But who would want to settle for permanent drought?

There is more to the problem of spiritual drought than its capacity to teach us valuable lessons. Secret sin abounds in times of spiritual drought. Coldness and formality replace living faith. Ecclesiastical power moves into the vacuum created by the absence of spiritual power. The church grows cold, worldly and sinful while in the world iniquity and lawlessness grow more and more.

Such is the time we live in. Revival? Yes, there are signs of it all over the world. But there are signs, too, that the "great wrath" of the devil is seen against mankind as never before. Flames of rage consume the earth. Terrorism and oppression, famine, war and death are merely symptoms of the devil's sadistic designs on the human race. Defiance kicks decent laws into its garbage heap and crushes God's standards beneath a booted heel. Human beings the world over are caught in sin's trap. We drink one another's blood and find pleasure in doing so, growing deaf and blind to the agony of the oppressed.

So we must pray. At such a time as this God's response has always been to pour out his Spirit upon his people. We must come on our faces before him. We must let his own sorrow and wrath produce travail in our spirits, travail that is unable to desist until we cry: "Send your Spirit, Lord! Baptize us anew with your power! Baptize me personally! Equip me for warfare and let your kingdom come on earth!"

The Cosmic Battle

The warfare on earth, as terrible and widespread as it is, is merely part of a larger cosmic warfare. Nowhere is its climax portrayed more vividly than in the nineteenth and twentieth chapters of Revelation. In blood-dipped clothing the King of kings rides a white charger. He is about to conquer the world in a horrifying battle, when he will tread down "the winepress of the fury of the wrath of God Almighty" (Rev 19:15).

Coming against him are the armies of the world led by the Beast and the False Prophet. The Beast seems to symbolize the tyranny and the godlessness of human government. The False Prophet represents false religion, always the ally of corrupt government. He has helped to entrench the power of the Beast by performing miracles and signs that have deceived the people. Both Beast and Prophet are captured in the battle and flung into the lake of fire.

We must notice two things about the scenario. John is giving us the obverse side of earthbound political structures. Human government is at once the God-given means by which lawlessness is held in check and that mechanism of rebellion by which we supplant

God's government. In Romans 13 Paul sees government as God's sovereign kindness to us. In Revelation John sees it as our alliance with the prince of this world.

We think of most modern governments as secular. The secularism is illusion, as is the charade of civic religion enacted by some western political leaders. No country in the world is immune from the danger of being governed by the Beast and the False Prophet, and Christians in the West are in grave danger of being fooled by them. It is power that interests most political leaders. And Satan has it to offer. Throughout history kings, emperors and presidents have been eager to acquire it from whatever source. Beast and False Prophet are once more cheek by jowl.

So the battle, the battle by which the King of kings finally establishes unopposed rule, is already in progress. It is a battle that has ebbed and flowed for centuries. Its tempo is now quickening. Not all scholars agree about what John is saying, or on the literal fulfillment of his words. But let us assume for a moment that dark powers will one day coalesce their forces behind a supreme human False Prophet, and an ultimate expression of corrupt secular power. What we must realize is that the scenario will merely be the final chapter of the story our own lives are now a part of.

We already have the Beast. He exists wherever there is tyrannical government. False prophets have abounded in history, and more and more are producing wonders and signs. History also gives us examples of the alliance between the two. Witch doctors can be allied to cruel tribal chiefs, magicians to Pharaohs, priests of Baal with a Jezebel, and a Grigori Rasputin with an Empress Alexandra. Always behind the alliances are the powers of darkness. Earthly events merely reflect the warfare in the heavenlies.

The Old Testament rings with battle cries and clashing weapons. Yet even in the Old Testament there are glimpses of the real locus of war. Battles on earth were won or lost in spiritual regions. How, for instance, could Elisha escape the army of Aram sent out to capture him in Dothan? Aram surrounded the city with chariots and horsemen. But Elisha's servant saw the secret of his master's tranquility. The surrounding hills were ringed with fiery horses and chariots. There were legions at Elisha's disposal, legions for whose weapons earth's forces had no countermeasures (2 Kings 6:8-23). Joshua was taught the same lesson when the Commander of the Lord's armies (on foot on that occasion and not riding a white horse) assailed him (Josh 5:13—6:5).

The demonic forces that will ultimately empower the Beast and the False Prophet with him are currently active in many human leaders and institutions. And when God calls us to do battle with demonic miracle-working powers, we shall need the empowering of the Spirit and the whole armor of God.

The Danger of Indecision
There are times when it is unwise to postpone decisions. If you live on the banks of a rising river you certainly do not want to evacuate your house before real danger of flood is present. But on the other hand, you do not want to be caught leaving at the last moment when muddy waters suddenly start pouring into your basement. Rivers in flood do not wait for your convenience. They follow their own timetable.

God's dealings in history are dealings in time. They begin and they end. Once they begin they do not wait for us to make up our minds about them. The drama enacts itself according to eternal purposes.

The tide of battle is rising fast. The fires of revival seem to be already on their way. Time and tide, as an old proverb puts it, wait for no man. Or, as Shakespeare expresses it more elegantly,

> There is a tide in the affairs of men, Which taken at flood leads on to fortune; Omitted, all the voyage of their life Is bound in shallows and in miseries.[4]

I would hesitate to say that those Christians who are bypassed by the floodtide of revival are always doomed to shallows and to miseries. Nevertheless, this has been the fate of many Christians who shrank back from previous revivals. Some were caught up by God in spite of their hesitation, or, as we have seen, in spite of their hostility and opposition. But they were the exceptions. For others the voyage of their lives was thereafter bound (even though in the world's eyes a few of them might have sailed to fame and fortune) in shallow lagoons and empty spiritual backwaters.

One need not do anything if one finds it hard to make up one's mind. One can read as well as pray. There are the Scriptures and there are books that bear on the subject. There are also a number of movements of prayer for worldwide revival.

I know, of course, that there are some who in their fear or their pride seem to be entrenched in hostility toward the things I have been talking about. This is sad. Jonathan Edwards's words to his contemporaries should not be forgotten:

Those who stand wondering at this strange work, not knowing what to make of it, and refusing to receive it—and ready . . . to speak contemptibly of it, as was the case of the Jews of old— would do well to . . . tremble at St. Paul's word . . . "Beware therefore lest that come upon you, which is spoken of in the prophets, Behold, ye despisers, and wonder, and perish; for I work a work in your days, which you shall in no wise believe, though a man declare it unto you." . . . Let all to whom this work is a cloud and darkness—as the pillar of cloud and fire was to the Egyptians—take heed that it be not their destruction, while it gives light to God's Israel.[5]

Notes

Chapter 1. What in the World Is God Doing?

[1]As quoted in J. Sidlow Baxter, *Divine Healing of the Body* (Grand Rapids, Mich.: Zondervan, 1979), p. 87.

[2]Jonathan Edwards, "A Faithful Narrative of a Surprising Work of God," in *The Works of Jonathan Edwards*, vol. 1 (Edinburgh: Banner of Truth, 1974), p. 354.

Chapter 2. Has It Ever Happened Before?

[1]For a fuller discussion of the revival in Nehemiah 8, see John White, *Excellence in Leadership* (Downers Grove, Ill.: InterVarsity Press, 1986), pp. 105-15.

[2]Jonathan Parsons, as quoted in Arnold A. Dallimore, *George Whitefield*, vol. 2 (Westchester, Ill.: Crossway Books, 1980), p. 183.

[3]Blaise Pascal, *Pensees*, Section four A.

[4]W. R. Moody, *The Life of D. L. Moody* (New York: Fleming H. Revell, 1900), p. 149.

[5]George Jeffreys, *Healing Rays* (London: Elim, 1935), p. 55.

[6]Sydney Ahlstrom, *A Religious History of the American People* (New Haven, Conn.: Yale University Press, 1972), pp. 286-87.

Chapter 3. Revival Rejected

[1]Oscar Cullman, *Christ and Time* (London: S.C.M., 1951), p. 64.

[2]Jonathan Edwards, *The Works of Jonathan Edwards*, vol. 2 (Edinburgh: Banner of Truth, 1974), p. 273.

[3]Ibid., p. 264.

[4]Ibid., p. 265.

[5]Arnold A. Dallimore, *George Whitefield*, vol. 1 (Westchester, Ill.: Crossway, 1980), p. 333.

[6]D. Martyn Lloyd-Jones, *Joy Unspeakable: Power and Renewal in the Holy Spirit* (Wheaton, Ill.: Harold Shaw, 1985), p. 51.

[7]Dallimore, vol. 2, p. 131.

[8]Vinson Synan, *The Holiness-Pentecostal Movement in the United States* (Grand Rapids, Mich.: Eerdmanns, 1971), pp. 143-44.

[9]Beverly Carradine, *A Box of Treasure* (Chicago, 1910), pp. 78-85, as quoted by Synan, p. 145.

[10]G. Campbell Morgan, as quoted by Synan, p. 145.

[11]J. B. Simpson, as quoted by Synan, p. 145.

[12]John Wesley, The Works of John Wesley, vol. 1 (Peabody, Mass: Hendrickson, 1872; rpt. 1984), p. 185.

[13]Edwards, vol. 2, p. 261.

[14]Friend George, as quoted by Dallimore, vol. 2, p. 89.

[15]George Whitfield, as quoted by Dallimore, vol. 2, pp. 89-90.

[16]Ibid., p. 125.

[17]D. Martyn Lloyd-Jones, The Sovereign Spirit: Discerning His Gifts (Wheaton, Ill.: Harold Shaw, 1985), p. 56.

[18]Edwards, vol. 1, p. 367.

[19]Edwards, vol. 2, p. 271.

[20]Ibid.

[21]Ibid.

[22]John Wimber, Power Evangelism (London: Hodder and Stoughton; and San Francisco: Harper & Row, 1985), p. 32.

[23]Ibid., pp. 35-36.

[24]An "instance of glossolalia in London occurred in 1875 when Dwight L. Moody preached at a Y.M.C.A. meeting at the Victoria Hall. After speaking to a small group of men in an afternoon service, Moody left the group 'on fire' with the young men 'speaking with tongues' and 'prophesying.' In a sense Moody could be classified as a pre-pentecostal preacher, although tongues could not be said to have characterized his revival services. This instance, however, indicated that glossolalia sometimes accompanied his preaching." Synan, The Holiness Pentecostal Movement, pp. 98-99, is here citing Walter J. Hollenweger, "Handbuch Der Pfingstbewegung" (unpublished doctoral dissertation, University of Zurich, 1965), II, 360, and suggests also John C. Pollock, Moody (New York: Macmillan, 1963), pp. 90-91.

[25]Iain H. Murray, David Martyn Lloyd-Jones (Edinburgh: The Banner of Truth Trust, 1982), p. 68.

Chapter 4. Should We Fear Emotions?

[1]Arnold A. Dallimore, George Whitefield, vol. 2 (Westchester, Ill.: Crossway, 1980), p. 130. Dallimore goes on to quote Macfarlan: "It is not alleged . . . that there is any virtue in such bodily manifestations. . . . [But] the mother weeps, and it may be faints, over the loss of a beloved child; the mercantile adventurer is distracted on hearing of some heavy and overwhelming loss; and the condemned criminal is removed from the bar agitated and convulsed; and is there anything unnatural in the tears, or even in strong bodily agitation on his part, who has just been brought to see that his soul, as well as his body, is in a lost, and, as it appears to him, a hopeless condition?" (p. 130).

[2]Jonathan Edwards, "A Treatise Concerning Religious Affections" in The Works of Jonathan Edwards, vol. 1 (Edinburgh: The Banner of Truth Trust, 1974), p.

243.
[3]Ibid., p. 238.
[4]Ibid.
[5]"There never was anything considerable brought to pass in the heart or life of any man living, by the things of religion, that had not his heart deeply affected by those things." Ibid., p. 237.
[6]Ibid., p. 237.
[7]Ibid.
[8]Ibid.
[9]Ibid.
[10]John Wesley, *The Works of John Wesley*, 3rd ed., vol. 1 (Peabody, Mass.: Hendrickson, 1872; rpt. 1984), p. 103.
[11]D. Martyn Lloyd-Jones, *Joy Unspeakable* (Wheaton, Ill.: Harold Shaw, 1985), p. 18.

Chapter 5. Are Revival Experiences Psychological?

[1]Charles T. Tart, *Altered States of Consciousness* (Garden City, N.Y.: Anchor, 1969).
[2]Charles Wesley, as quoted in Arnold A. Dallimore, *George Whitefield*, vol. 1 (Westchester, Ill.: Crossway, 1980), p. 326.
[3]Dallimore, vol. 1, p. 325.
[4]John White, *The Golden Cow* (Downers Grove, Ill.: InterVarsity Press, 1979).
[5]John White, *Flirting with the World* (Wheaton, Ill.: Harold Shaw, 1982), pp. 113-25.
[6]Douglas R. Groothuis, *Unmasking the New Age* (Downers Grove, Ill.: InterVarsity Press, 1985), p. 24.
[7]Louis Linn, M.D., as quoted in Harold A. Kaplan and Benjamin J. Sadock, eds., *Comprehensive Textbook of Psychiatry*, 4th ed. (Baltimore: Williams and Wilkins, 1985), p. 567.
[8]Charles A. Johnson, *The Frontier Camp Meeting* (Dallas: Southern Methodist University Press, 1955), p. 55.
[9]James B. Finley, as quoted in Johnson, pp. 64-65.
[10]Henry Venn, as quoted in Dallimore, vol. 2, pp. 392-93.

Chapter 6. Are Revival Experiences Spiritual?

[1]Jonathan Edwards, *The Works of Jonathan Edwards*, vol. 2 (Edinburgh: The Banner of Truth, 1974), p. 265.
[2]John Wesley, *The Works of John Wesley*, vol. 1 (Peabody, Mass.: Hendrickson, 1872; rpt. 1984), pp. 234, 236.
[3]John Cennick, as quoted in Arnold A. Dallimore, *George Whitefield*, vol. 1, (Westchester, Ill.: Crossway, 1980), p. 327.
[4]Ralph Humphries, as quoted in Dallimore, vol. 1, p. 326.
[5]Wesley, vol. 1, p. 190.

244WHEN THE SPIRIT COMES WITH POWER ◆

[6]Ibid., pp. 36-37.
[7]Edwards, vol. 2, p. 261.
[8]Ibid., pp. 257-77.

Chapter 7. Varieties of Revival Experiences

[1]Rudolph Otto, The Idea of the Holy (New York: Oxford University Press, 1950), pp. 8-9.
[2]Ibid., p. 10.
[3]Ibid., p. 13.
[4]Edwards, vol. 1, p. 238.
[5]Alexander Webster, as quoted in Dallimore, vol. 2, p. 128.
[6]Edwards, p. 348.
[7]Ibid., vol. 2, p. 407.
[8]John Hamilton, as quoted in Dallimore, vol. 1, p. 123.
[9]Dallimore, vol. 2, pp. 129-30.
[10]Edwards, vol. 1, p. 354.
[11]Ibid., p. 367.
[12]Quoted in Charles A. Johnson, The Frontier Camp Meeting (Dallas: Southern Methodist Press, 1955), p. 60.
[13]Edwards, vol. 1, p. 376.

Chapter 8. Why Do Revival Experiences Differ So Much?

[1]D. Martyn Lloyd-Jones, as quoted in Iain H. Murray, David Martyn Lloyd-Jones (Edinburgh: The Banner of Truth Trust), pp. 145-46.
[2]For a thorough statistical analysis of the reliability of words of knowledge at a conference led by John Wimber, see David C. Lewis, "Signs and Wonders in Sheffield: A Social Anthropologist's Analysis of Words of Knowledge, Manifestations of the Spirit, and the Effectiveness of Divine Healing" in John Wimber, Power Healing (San Francisco: Harper & Row, 1987), pp. 248-69.
[3]J. B. Rhine was a researcher at Duke in the 1940s and 1950s who performed a series of carefully controlled experiments in paranormal phenomena demonstrating that some people had ESP.
[4]John White, "Commentary on Psychological Observations on Demonism," in John Warwick Montgomery, ed., Demon Possession (Minneapolis: Bethany, 1976), pp. 252-55. These are the collected papers of the 1975 Notre Dame conference.
[5]See Sandy Solomon's story, chapter 13.

Chapter 9. How Safe Is Spiritual Power?

[1]John Wesley, The Works of John Wesley, 3rd ed., vol. 12 (Peabody, Mass.: Hendrickson, 1872; rpt. 1984), p. 106.
[2]Ibid., vol. 1, p. 188.
[3]Arnold A. Dallimore, George Whitefield, vol. 1 (Westchester, Ill.: Crossway,

1980), p. 309.
[4]John Cennick, as quoted in Dallimore, p. 326.
[5]Ibid., pp. 327-28.
[6]Jonathan Edwards, The Works of Jonathan Edwards, vol. 1 (Edinburgh: The Banner of Truth Trust, 1974), p. 371.

Chapter 10. Stolen Power
[1]Moses David Berg quoted in Deborah Davis, The Children of God (Grand Rapids, Mich.: Zondervan, 1982), p. 86.
[2]Quoted in Iain H. Murray, David Martyn Lloyd-Jones (Edinburgh: The Banner of Truth Trust), p. 221.
[3]Ibid., p. 239.
[4]John and Paula Sandford, The Elijah Task (Tulsa, Okla.: Victory House, 1977), p. 3.
[5]For an interesting first-person account of a "rape" by the powers of darkness, see Johanna Michaelson, The Beautiful Side of Evil (Eugene, Oreg.: Harvest House, 1982).
[6]Edwards, vol. 2, pp. 266-69.
[7]George Gallup, as quoted by Wimber, p. 48.

Chapter 11. John Wimber: Pandemonium in the School Gymnasium?
[1]From an unpublished manuscript by John Wimber and Kevin Springer.
[2]This account is also taken from an unpublished manuscript by John Wimber and Kevin Springer. The account of the man with the sandwich board also appears in John Wimber and Kevin Springer, Power Evangelism (London: Hodder and Stoughton; and San Francisco, Calif.: Harper & Row, 1985), pp. 13-14.
[3]The story of John Wimber's journey from being very opposed to healing to his eventual, but very reluctant, acceptance of it is a long one, told more fully in John Wimber and Kevin Springer, Power Healing (London: Hodder and Stoughton; and San Francisco, Calif.: Harper & Row, 1986).
[4]David Watson, Fear No Evil (Wheaton, Ill.: Harold Shaw, 1984), p. 25.
[5]D. Martyn Lloyd-Jones, Joy Unspeakable (Wheaton, Ill.: Harold Shaw, 1985), pp. 121-22.

Chapter 12. John Wimber and the Vineyard Movement
[1]Eddie Gibbs, "John Wimber—A Friend Who Causes Me to Wonder," Renewal, June-July 1986, p. 16.
[2]John Cennick, as quoted in Arnold A. Dallimore, George Whitefield, vol. 1 (Westchester, Ill.: Crossway, 1979), pp. 325-26.
[3]John Wesley, The Works of John Wesley, 3rd ed., vol. 1 (Peabody, Mass.: Hendrickson, 1872; rpt. 1984), p. 170.
[4]W. R. Moody, The Life of D. L. Moody (New York: Fleming H. Revell, 1900), p. 149.

[5]Op. cit., p. 153.
[6]Evelyn Underhill, Mysticism (New York: Meridian, World Publishing, 1955), p. 274.
[7]Tim Stafford, "Testing the Wine from John Wimber's Vineyard," Christianity Today, 8 August 86, p. 22.

Chapter 13. Sandy: The Voice on the Stereo
[1]D. Martyn Lloyd-Jones, The Sovereign Spirit (Wheaton, Ill.: Harold Shaw, 1985), pp. 96-98.

Chapter 14. Conrad: Drugs and a Demon
[1]I met Conrad in Calgary (Alberta, Canada) in September 1986. He told me his story over dinner in a hotel, and later wrote the story out for me. I received confirmation of the written details from his wife, another written account from his friend Mark, and further confirmation from conversations with Ken Blue.

Chapter 15. Jim: Power Encounter
[1]The account is taken (with Jim Hylton's permission) from an unpublished manuscript of his reflections on revival, The Shaking of Awakening, pp. 146-48.
[2]D. Martyn Lloyd-Jones, Joy Unspeakable (Wheaton, Ill.: Harold Shaw, 1985), p. 119.

Chapter 16. Preparing for Revival
[1]Andrew Murray, With Christ in the School of Prayer (Westwood, N.J.: Revell, 1953), p. 88.
[2]Joyce Huggett, The Joy of Listening to God (Downers Grove, Ill.: InterVarsity Press, 1986).
[3]Matthew Henry, Commentary on the Whole Bible (Grand Rapids, Mich.: Zondervan, 1961), p. 1628.
[4]William Shakespeare, Henry VIII, IV, iii, 217.
[5]Jonathan Edwards, The Works of Jonathan Edwards, vol. 1 (Edinburgh: The Banner of Truth Trust, 1974), p. 272.

Scripture Index

Name and Subject Index

249